Through It All I've Always Laughed

(An autobiography of myself)

by

Count Arthur Strong - The well known Celebrity.

Bold that up !!
Bigger as well

fff

FABER & FABER *and Faber !*
Shoddy !!!

fill this up with something

FRONTISPIECE

I don't really know what a 'Frontispiece' is? Or if that's how you spell it? Or if we're having one? No one's said anything to me. Is it where you get someone people will know to write something nice about you? Because if it is, I might get Barry Cryer to do it? For a fiver or something? He could make something up. Get back to me on that. I'll move on. You'll have to pay the fiver by the way. That'll not be coming out of my wages for doing this. If you can call it 'wages'.

get a red pen

AN INTRODUCTION

BY

COUNT ARTHUR STRONG - THE AUTHOR HIMSELF

Good afternoon. Firstly, can I thank you for
purchasing this book. I'm sure it will prove to
be a wise investment. Books do accrue in value
and some of THE BOOKS OF Charles's Dickenses,
for instance, can exchange hands for a nice bit
of money. If you're not buying it, and you've no
intention of buying it, and you're just looking
through it because it's raining outside and
you're early for the opticians, would you mind
putting it neatly back on the shelf please,
because you're spoiling it for someone else by
thumbing all the pages and everything. I never
buy the book at the front of the pile because
of that. I take the third or fourth one. Also,
some people don't wash their hands when they've
been to the toilet. And that's not a very nice
thought to have in your head when you're buying
a book. I remember reading in the paper that you

shouldn't eat the nuts that they put in a bowl, in a bar because other people might not wash their hands after they've 'paid a visit'. In fact in this article, it said they tested the nuts off a bar and found traces of twenty eight different types of urine in the bowl. So if you're reading this and you haven't washed your hands after urinating, then I think you should do the decent thing and purchase this wonderful book.

You know, when the people at Faber and Faber and Faber signed me up to write this memoir, I only had one stipulation and that was that in this book I would set out to write the truth. This book wouldn't be a dressed up version of events. This book would tell it like it was. This book would have Oliver Cromwell's warts and all in it.

But at the same time I wanted this book to be more than Oliver Cromwell's warts. I wanted this book to be a guide for people embarking on the showbiz journey. An aid. But not a manual of do's and don't's for aspiring performers, like Peter Barkworth's now sadly very dated book, 'About Acting', once was, once. Whilst I like Peter, and applaud him for what he was trying to do, that's

just too rigid a format for someone like I am (me).
So what I'll try to do, after I've been to Lidl's, is *pickled onions*
write from the heart, with the great honesty and
humility that's got me where I am today.

I've been very lucky in my life in that I've
probably achieved everything I set out to do and
very much more on top of all that. If someone
would have told me when I was a baby that one
day I would have been in close proximity to the
Queen Mother, accidentally standing on one of
her bunions, I would, quite frankly, have looked
at them as though they were mad. If I could have
understood what they were saying to me. I must
admit, I'm never quite sure how much a baby can
understand. Some of them look quite bright, as
if they know what's going on, yet others look as
though they haven't got a clue. For arguments
sake, let's say I was amongst the former, that did
have a clue.

Now, there are many, many people to thank for
helping me with this book. My wonderufl editor,
who's name has just escaped me for the moment,
without who's tireless help this book wouldn't
have been half the book it is/was. Barry Cryer

for his encyclopaedic memory. Thanks Barry! The drinks are on me! (No they're not. I'm joking). I wish I could mention them all but honestly the list is just to, to long to remember anyone.

Before I leave you though, I'd just like to say this, and that is, that in this profession that I've spent my life in, I have been blessed to have two of the most wonderful parents someone like me, or indeed 'me', because that's what I meant, could have. It was whilst under their care and guidance that I flourished and grew. They nurtured me as you would a flower and I bloomed and turned into the huge plant that stands before you today. So I'd just like to say a thank you to my Mamma and Father, wherever they went. Without them this book would not have been possible. It goes without saying that if they hadn't met I would have not been conceived. I suppose I might have been conceived by one of them with someone else, but I would have been quite different. For instance I could have been a woman. I suppose if they'd not met each other and had a baby with two different people, there could have been two of me, with half of me each in them, wandering around. However, sadly for me, they did meet and there is only one of me, I think.

So, sit back everybody, get your glasses on, open this book, (I know you've already opened it, but you know what I mean), and laugh, cry and the other one, at the sometime hilarious, sometime touching and sometime moving, but always entertaining collection of my life's lives lives's? memories.

Could I just say before I stop typing this, if you enjoy the book, and frankly, there'd have to be something wrong with you if you didn't, could I ask you not to lend it on to a friend, or give it to the charity shop? Because that would only mean that someone wouldn't buy it at full price. And that's not very nice for me if you flood the market with cheap used ones. Also lending the book on to someone could lead to a wider urine/ hygiene problem, as outlined earlier. So I am really thinking of other people.

Anyway, whatever happens everybody, one thing's for sure, everybody, 'Through It All I've always Laughed'.

And I've got the title in!

[7]

PREFACE

Are we having a preface? I'll move on for now.

what is a preface?

CHAPTER ONE

THE EARLY YEARS!

"Wah! Wah!" Went the cries of the one minute old new born baby.

Had the midwife possessed a tuning fork she would be able to tell you that this precociously talented child, by now some one minute and thirty seconds old, had hit a pitch perfect top 'C'. A talent I still possess to this day.

For you see, I was this small precocious and, by now, pushing two minute old child. But perhaps I should explain to you how this miracle birth came to be. Let me take you back in time to a night some nine months prior to the birth of myself.

Ginger nuts
Cabbage
bacon
stamps

Mother and Father, as I called them, were in pantomime at the Watford Palace doing a dog act. After the act they went home and had sexual relations. And that's how a baby like I was is born.

He was always good with dogs was Father. I
think that's why he married my Mother. She had
a nice cocker spaniel. A ginger and white one
called Nuts. I don't know why she called it that.
Perhaps it liked nuts? There's nothing wrong
with that. I like a nut myself. Apart from Brazil
nuts, ever since I had a chocolate Brazil stuck
in my throat in 1960 something, which led to a
near death experience. Luckily for me though,
I coughed it up and finished eating it. Not the
last time I would go on to cheat death.

Anyway, that Mother and Father would meet,
fall in love and form a dog act, was inevitable
and they enjoyed some moderate success on the
variety circuit.

However, when I came along that fateful day that
changed the course of so many people's lives,
myself included, it was decided that Father would
go solo and do an act of his own, until Mother
recovered from my birth and her stitches healed
up, because of my hat size.

The act Dad decided to do, was playing the
'William Tell Overture' by hitting himself on the
head with a mallet, with two cymbals strapped

[12]

to his knees. After a few performances though
he realised that he hadn't quite thought it
through properly, and he had to stop, because it
quite hurt and he kept blacking out and he was
spending a lot of time in casualty.

However worse was to come. Much, much, much, much
worse. And I make no apologies for using 'much' a
lot in that sentence, because it was much worse.
Much, much, much, much, much worse.

I'm very pleased with this bit

In 1939 Adolf Hitler started the war. Why? Well
we can only guess at that. He must have been
absolutely mad.

Carried away with the thrill of it all, my Dad
enlisted as soon as the magistrate made him. My
Mother, as I called her, was left on her own at a
very vulnerable time.

Now everybody, If you're not already sitting down,
I want you to sit down for this bit, because what
I'm about to tell you next will be a huge sock to
you and I don't want you to keel over then send
me a solicitor's letter making out I did it.

What it is is that I later learnt that whilst
my Father, or 'Dad' as I sometimes called him, I

disguises for Hitler.

forget which now, was off 'hanging his washing on the Seigfried Line', that my mother took solace in the arms of another -- a variety turn called 'Wee Billy Bugle and his Hoop of Flames', or Uncle Willy as I came to know him as.

Oh, he could make that bugle talk could Billy and he was always very good to me, God rest his soul. He's no longer with us. I remember his last words as though it was tomorrow. "Put me out! I'm on flipping fire".

Uncle Willy went up like a bazooka. They do say there's still some bits of him on the ceiling at the Bradford Alhambra. They haven't the heart to clean him off. Or a long enough ladder, if truth be known.

Anyway, all I know is, he was like an Uncle to me was Uncle Willy. *Stamp*

With Dad away at the Maginot line, or whatever it is, and Uncle Willy all over, firstly my mother, and secondly the Alhambra ceiling, things were very hard for us. I helped as well as I could, tried not to cry too much and soiled as few nappies as was physically possible.

The war years were terribly, terribly hard for a
young child like myself and all the other people
in the country too. Every night when I went to
bed I could only pray that the war would last
another eighteen years so that I could sign up
and fly a Spitfire, like Kenneth Moore did in
that film about Douglas Bader's Bouncing Bombs.
But at the moment I had more pressing things to
do, like learn to walk. *↑ (!) That might not be true*

You'll be happy to know that through my dogged
perseverance and a few false starts, I did learn
to walk, and to this day it's something I still
have great sucsess succsess suscess success
doing. So stick that up your pipe and smoke
it Mr Hitler! While the Blitzkrieg raged this
precocious talent, writing this, was getting on
with it!

During these war years I took great solace
in all the postcards my father managed to
hurriedly pencil. I still couldn't read, obviously,
but I used to like ripping them up and chewing
them etcetera. I would wait by the letterbox
for the postman and rip anything up that came
through. Mother would sometimes lose her temper
Remember picture of cat mess on path. Mr Ellis

with me but I was a beautiful, lovely child and *Hazel!* *Do possib* *blue*
would just look at her with my big . ... eyes and
any anger she felt would melt away. Plus most of
the time now she was on the gin.

After Uncle Willy had blown up, there was only
Mother to support the two of us and she needed a
new act. She'd heard there was a job going with a
contortionist in Doncaster. So we packed our bags
and moved up there, to stop with my Auntie Irene.

Being a contortionist really suited mother and
I don't think I've ever seen her as happy as when
she was bent over backwards doing the splits and
eating grapes with two dislocated arms. She had
always been supple. In fact she could still sit
on the floor at ninety. Which was remarkable ...
She couldn't get up mind.

She always looked younger than she was, did *Guinne Book of Record*
Mother. In fact we're all like that in my family.
My Uncle Earnest looked like a toddler right
up into his seventies. We all look younger. We've
all got elastic skin, like my Mother had. Oh yes.
I've never had any of my buttocks siphoned off
and squirted in my forehead like some of them,
thank you very much! Cliff Richards has it done

[16] *Stamps*

once a fortnight! It's a wonder he can sit down.
His bottom must be red raw some nights. Lulu,
she's another one. Oh dear. It would be dreadful
if they got the syringes mixed up and you ended
up with Cliff Richards buttocks in your face.
I wouldn't know where to put myself. I mean I
liked, 'Mistletoe and Wine', but I wouldn't want his
buttocks in my face.

Count Arthur Strong

Best Wishes!

Arthur

Arthur x Count Arthur Strong

A

Gracious

I accept this award with gracious thanks! Thank you so much!

CHAPTER THREE

MISSING PRESUMED DEAD!

I'll never forget the day that telegram *check date*
came . . . 'Missing presumed dead' it said. Which,
coincidentally, is what this chapter is called, if
you look at the top of the page. I wondered where
I'd heard it before. Mother opened the envelope,
read the contents, then howled like a 'ban shea'.

'Why! Why!', she shrieked! 'Why! has this happened
to us'? She sunk to the floor with her head in
her hands, (a variation of this move she would
later use to great success in the act). 'Curse you
Adolph Hitler! Curse you!' I had never seen the
old girl like this before and I consoled her as
best as a just coming up to one year old that
couldn't speak could.

It was this day that I resolved, that even if
this accursed war lasted until armistice day on
the 14 August 1945, I would not rest until I had
brought Hitler to book at Nuremberg.

Hitler! The very word would bring me out in
nappy rash. It still does. I would imagine him
stood at the other end of where the channel
tunnel might come out, if it'd been invented then,
hands on hips, head tossed back, laughing like
a hyena while we starved. Eating a three course
meal of, perhaps, Prawn Cocktail to start with,
followed by maybe a nice bit of Liver and Onions
with Apple Pie and custard for his pudding, or *ground*
perhaps rhubarb? The unfairness of this was not *nutmeg*
lost on me despite my tender years. Or year. *on tap*

And so here I was, the Fatherless son of a
contortionist Mother. One year old, living in war
torn Doncaster, in the South Riding of Yorkshire,
starving for some dinner.

In later years I would immortalise this moment
in song, set to the music of Ronnie Conway. Not
his real name. He made it up because he thought
it made him sound big. Which I think is a little
bit sad. And when I say, 'set to the music, of
Ronnie Conway', I actually hummed and la'd all
the tune to him to start with. Something that
he consistently chooses to ignore as he travels *Skegness*
around most of Lincolnshire, making a fortune *Ingomells*
off the back of my back.

Stamp

And if I wasn't involved in an ongoing copyright
dispute with Ronnie (or Colin as his real name
is) at the moment, I was going to put that song
up for the Eurovision Song Contest. So it's
highly likely Ronnie Colin is responsible for
us not winning that as well for the last fifty
years.

Anyway, my contact at the Citizens Advice says
he can't stop me reproducing the lyrics for your
enjoyment, because I am the sole lyricist of it.
The song in question is just below this sentence
you're just finishing reading. It's called
'Doncaster'.

Doncaster!
A small talented child in . . .
Doncaster!
Afraid and alone in . . .
Doncaster!
Laughed at because of the posh way I talk in . . .
Doncaster!
At the house of my Auntie Irene in . . .
Doncaster!

(spoken bridge)
Please don't make me eat tripe Aunty Irene,
I promise I'll be good!
(now back to singing it)

And then like a flower that blooms in the garden,
I bend in the breeze,
That blows through the trees, in . . .
Doncaster!
A man can walk tall in . . .
Doncaster!
Your worries are small in . . .
Doncaster! In . . .
Doncaster! In . . .
Doncaster!

Mention they can buy the VD!

And incidentally everyone, I have recently been
in communication with someone who will have to
remain nameless, for obvious reasons, about them
releasing that song out in time for Christmas
one year. Because I think it could be as big a
hit as 'Candle in the Window' was for him. And I'm
expecting a reply any day now, to my stamped,
self address letter I sent to him, c/o Watford
Football Club, where he is the goalkeeper.

Stamps

So when Elvis John finally deigns to get back
to me, I might not have to finish this book,
should 'Doncaster' go to number one in the hit
parade and I make millions. Which I apologise
in advance for, if you've bought it and are
disappointed because it stops suddenly.

But I digress. For a naturally inquisitive,
talented and precocious posh sounding posh   *Posh*
small child like I was, wartime Doncaster wasn't
all all bad news, and growing up around the
variety theatres of the north proved to be
the making of me, although I didn't know it at
the time. And frankly, if you'd tried to tell me
that at the age of one and a bit I would have
probably told you that you were mad. If, A, I
could have talked, or B, I could have understood
what you were going on about in the first place,
in the first place.   *Shoes*

It took Mother a long while to get over the bad
news about Father and for a time she turned to
spiritualism to try to ascertain once and for
all whether Father was dead or alive or had just
deserted again.

I had always had, 'special feelings', shall I call

Stamps

them, that I was not alone and could see through walls and read minds etcetera, like Doris Stokes does. Or did, if she's dead. Mother was aware that I was attuned in to the 'other side'. By the 'other side' I don't mean ITV. I mean the spirit world. Which I always think would be a good name for an Off License. 'Spiritworld'. It's nearly as good as 'Bargain Booze'. Anyway, sometimes mother would use me as a spirit guide at her seances I forgot to tell you about.

I recall at one such seance channeling the spirit of Henry the Eighth, and do you know to this day I can still remember his eight wives off by heart, without even thinking about it. Anne Boleyn, Anne of Cleaves, Ann of a thousand days, Katherine of Argon, Katherine Parr, Katherine Hepburn, Audrey Hepburn, Felicity Kendall and Glenda Rogers. There you are! That's at least seven. And Glenda Rogers is definite before you say anything, because she was on telly doing it with Keith Michel. *Bargain Hunt,*

So deep were these Mamma induced trances that the only thing that would bring me back from the spirit world was our parrot pecking me on

the head. I was very close to that parrot. In
fact I could probably remember it's name if I
put my mind to it, and was devastated that when
rationing bit deep, we had to eat him. With a few
of last nights potatoes. In fact even now when
times are hard I will talk to that pigeon as if
it's there, and I find this a great comfort. To
a point. Not pigeon, parrot. Pigeons can't talk.
Some people refer to them as vermin. In fact some
other people call them rats with tails. Or is that
squirrels? And what does that even mean? 'Rats
with tails?' Rats are rats with tails surely?
Squirrels are squirrels with tails. Pigeons don't
have tails. Only an idiot would go round saying
something like that. Plus, last time I looked
pigeons and squirrels don't talk. Apart from
'Tufty' who wasn't real.

Anyway, so here I was, the Fatherless son of
a contortionist Mother. One year old, living
in war torn Doncaster, in the South Riding of
Yorkshire, starving and parrotless. I remember
thinking what would life hold in store for me as
I approach chapter three of my book?

CHAPTER THREE OF MY BOOK

GROWING PAINS!

Listen, before I start chapter three, what about
this for an idea? A cookery book with all the
recipes from the Bible in it! The menu could have,

Lamb of God,   *Manna from Heaven?*
Fatted calf,
Fish with bread,   *Doner kebabs?*
Water into wine.
Doves.

Can you eat doves? Or does the Queen own them
all? Find that out. And there must be a kebab
recipe in the Bible? It's a big thick book. And how
many people go to church? Millions. And they all
eat.

Listen, instead of bread for communion we could
do little canapes. That's got to taste better than
bread? And anyway even if they don't like the
food they would have to turn the other cheek

wouldn't they? I could be dressed like Moses on
the cover! Holding a food mixer. Unleavened bread!
That's another one. Put that on the menu.

I'd quite like to have my own chain of
ecclesiastical restaurants? All done up with
church pews? We could even have a pulpit and an
altar in there? The font could be full of crabs
and lobsters. Then people could pick which one
they want to eat.

All the staff could be dressed like vicars for
the waiters, and nuns for the waitresses. The
manager could be dressed like the Archbishop
of Canterbury, and like I say I could be
Moses, because it's my idea. And I would be the
figurehead. Get back to me.

CHAPTER THREE AGAIN.

GROWING PAINS

"Owch! That hurt," was something I seemed to be saying more and more and more these days. Or those days, if you want to split hairs. Despite rationing, I was growing fast, like forced rhubarb does. Every three months my Mother, as I called her, bade me stand with my back to the wall and she would chalk my height up on it. Which was fine until they wallpapered, then nobody knew how tall I was anymore. I still don't know how tall I was as a child to this day.

By this time in the war, like most people, we had a pig and were growing all our own vegetables. Peas, Cauliflowers, potatoes, cucumbers, grapes, *carrots* turnips, cabbage, cress, and grapefruits, are just some of the vegetables I can remember. Swedes, beetroot, sprouts, apples, yams, advacados and porridge are some of the other ones I can also remember now I've had a look in a book. *Stamps*

As we approached that Christmas, father's absence

was beginning to tell on us. We'd always been inseparable, when he was there, and not knowing if he was alive or what, was taking a cruel toll on those left behind.

On Christmas eve I went to bed feeling very sorry for myself. Suddenly, as I was putting an old sock up, I heard loud voices downstairs. Seconds later, Mother burst excitedly into my bedroom.

"Darling if you could have one thing for Christmas, what would it be?", she ejaculated.

"Anything?" I asked her, tears forming like a misty day in my head where my eyes were.

"Anything", she repeated repeated.

Before I could answer, I heard an familiar cough on the staircase outside my bedroom door.

"Is that father come home mother?" I asked her, my voice just a croak in my throat.

"Yes! Yes! Yes!" she said three times.

"Yes", as she added a fourth.

"Has he got a parcel shaped like a bike with him?" I intoned, as father burst in to the

room and raced toward me. I soon got over the
disappointment of him being bike-less when he
gave me a collection of bottle tops off all the
different bottled beer he'd drunk since he'd been
missing. It was a comprehensive collection and
if I knew what had happened to them I would
cherish them to this day. Mother laughed gaily
like a young idiot, and we were, at last all
together again.

When we'd all calmed down, father explained his
absence to us. Apparently he'd been involved in
a secret mission behind enemy lines that only
Winston Churchill and the King knew about,
when a horrible, big German just came up to him
and for no reason at all shot him in the foot,
leaving my father in a total state of disbelief,
that something like that could happen in this
day and age.

He limped painfully back to the British lines.
But when he got there they callously accused
him of shooting himself in the foot to get out
of doing the war any more. Father protested his
innocence vehemently but they would have none
of it, citing the fact that his own bullet had
just been removed from his foot.

Anyway, in my young eyes my father had returned a hero. It mattered not to me that it was himself's foot he'd shot himself in. At least he'd shot something. He held me at arms length and looked at me.

"My goodness Arnold", he exclaimed, "Look at you, my boy. How you've grown. How tall are you?"

Alas I could only give him my height before we wallpapered, which I feared was by now out by a good two inches. If you're under the age of forty or you come from France or somewhere like that, and don't know what two inches is, look it up.

Doctor Baker
4 O'clock !!!
Take sample

CHAPTER

MOVING ON.

With pater at home once more and because of his
war wound unable to walk properly, apart from
inside the house, our life slowly began to return
to normal. Mother had built up quite a following
on the variety circuit with the act, so it was
decided that she should continue with that and
Father should just live off what she earned
until it was safe for him to walk properly
outside.

Dad was a jealous man by nature and he took
against one of the other contortionists in the
act 'Lennie Longarms', claiming that he kept
rubbing his hands up against Mother. Lennie was
a very talented individual and as his Variety
monica suggests he did have extraordinary long
arms. The things he could reach with those arms
of his was the stuff of legend. Ask Roy Hudd. I
myself, once saw him reach a bottle of tomato
sauce, true as I'm stood here, or sat here to be
accurate.

I should perhaps point out that the sauce was a long way away from him and again stress that there was abnormal length to his long arms.

The high point of his solo act was when he stood on the middle of the stage and pretended he had an itch on his back that he couldn't get to, to scratch. So he reached off into the wings, stage left and after a minute his arms reappeared stage right behind himself, and he scratched his back that way. Wonderful. Of course he had an assistant. Nobody's arms are that long.

It's a shame they don't have things like that on the telly any more. There's a right load of rubbish on. I was flicking with the pressit yesterday and there was hardly anything on worth watching. I'd seen the 'Wheeler Dealers' before, that was a repeat and David Dickinson's gone right down since he went over to ITV. They want to get me on that. Even the news was rubbish. I used to like it on the News at Ten when Terry McDonald always ended with a funny little story about a telegraph pole being stuck up a cat and the fire brigade coming out. Or a steam roller flattening a house when they're all in bed. Something you could have a bit of a laugh at. But now it's all terrible news. And all the news readers are sober. They want to get me on that. As for the politicians, Oh dear don't get me started on that. Have you noticed, it doesn't matter who the Prime Minister is, they all get on my nerves?

All that apart I was at the age of three or four about to enter the most salient point of my life.

CHAPTER 7 (I think)

MOVING ON MORE

I was, as I just intimated on the previous
page, approximately three or four years old
now, and as you would expect me to be, quite
a bit intellectually advanced for someone of
approximately that age. To give you a rough
guide to how clever I was, if say, The Sun
newspaper, had been around in those days, I
would estimate that I'd almost be able to finish
the crossword. By myself. Not that I buy The
Sun. I mean if there's one in the barbers I'll
have a look at it and maybe take it home if no
one's looking. But I wouldn't pay good money for
it.

You know, being a busy celebrity I can't be seen
to be favouring any one of the newspapers over
another. And I have to make no exception about
that rule. It's very important to me that I'm
not seen to be breaking the hypocratic oath
about that. Except the ones that have given me

nice reviews, obviously. Like The Telegraph, The
Independent, The Guardian, The Sunday Mail, The
Daily Mail, The Mirror, The Times and The Sunday
Times. The quality newspapers. I mean, you know,
you scratch my back and I'll scratch you back.
Which is fair enough. The rest of them can go
and stick there heads where the sun hurts. And
again I don't mean 'The Sun' as in the newspaper.
I mean the 'sun' as in the sky. It's just an
expression isn't it. 'Stick your head where the
sun hurts'. Everybody says it . . . Or something
similar to it.

Anyway, back to my story. My parents, wanting
the very best education possible for me,
enrolled me at the nearest school to where we
lived and at whatever age I would have been, on
whatever date it was - a Monday, I would presume.
If you're starting something normal people tend
to start on a Monday don't you? - I nervously
walked what seemed to me an endless thirty feet,
to what was to be my hallowed hall of academia
for the next however long I was there before we
left. I will look all that up. I have a cardboard
box somewhere with all that stuff in it. Photos
the lot.

Where is that box?

I arrived in good time that first day. Mother had packed me a satchel containing my writing slate and a stick of chalk, which she said I was not to eat. The chalk, not the slate. Who eats slate? . . . I suppose the Welsh might? That would make sense.

Ever since I was a small baby I'd like to eat chalk. I don't know why. But I do I think it has laxative qualities and I still have the odd stick now and again when I'm having a bit of trouble in that department. But this stick of chalk was for my writing slate and I followed Mothers instructions implicitly. And she didn't say I couldn't suck it did she?

It was on this first day at school that I had a chance meeting with someone which would change my life for a bit.

I'd only just gone through the school gates when I was greeted by the head boy. A small grey haired man with his trademark big glasses. I mean a small boy, not man. He's a man now that's why I said that but then he was a boy and a small one.

Get some chalk

Stamps

The name of that small man/boy was Barry Cryer
and although he was a few years older than me,
and looks it, he and I were to become a lifelong
friend of mine. Read on and find out more about
this by turning this page over.

This is a waste of paper

CHAPTER 7

MY SCHOOL DAYS

Despite the war, the next few years were the happiest days of my life, and I took to school like a duck. All the teachers loved teaching me because I was so receptive. My favourite lesson was on a Friday afternoon and you won't be surprised to hear that it was drama. They say you'll always remember a good teacher and our drama teacher was no exception. He was called something like Mr Parkinson. It wasn't that, but it was similar sounding and it's near enough for our purposes. I'll never forget him, whatever his name was.

Mrs Parkinson was a wonderful man and he was like a father figure to me. Borrowing money off me and getting me to go to the off license for him, to get his drink and Woodbines. In those days they didn't ask you to prove your age when you bought alcohol and fags, so most peoples children got all that sort of thing for their

tin of pease
sauce
cream craker
Liner
Stamps

dads. That's just one of the things that was better then. And you could leave your front door open. We used to. Alright, fair enough, the door was actually stolen eight or nine times, but they never set foot in the house. There was a line and people didn't used to step over it. Everyone knew everyone.

We knew who the bobby on the beat was as well. It was my Uncle George. Not like today. I can't think of a single policeman or policewoman that's a relative of mine today. How can that be progress?

My Uncle George would come down our street, pushing his bike twice a day, come rain or shine. Unless it was raining, and all the children would follow him and tell him they all wanted to be a policeman when they grew up. And he would give them a stick of chewing gum. Or candle wax during the war, when chewing gum was scarce. Now that's policing.

I had another piece of bad news that week. It was that my good but older than me friend Barry Cryer, was to leave the school to move to Leeds. In the few weeks I'd been there, despite the fact, as I've said that Barry was a good few

years older than me and looks it, he and I and I
had probably become inseparable. And I'll never
forget his tearstained face as I rather suavely
bade him farewell. I didn't get much time to dwell
on his departure for long though, because an
exciting new chapter of my life was about to
start which was a huge surprise to me. Read on
and find out what that chapter was in the next
chapter.

*Find Banny's
address!*

Loft?

CHAPTER 8?

THE NEXT CHAPTER

The next chapter in my life I'm talking about,
just for clarity, isn't what we've come to
understand by 'chapter' in this wonderful book.
It's a figure of speech and it means the next 'bit'
of my life. The next 'part' of my life. It's only
confusing because in books you have chapters.
And although this chapter is entitled, 'The Next
Chapter' it isn't what I meant. Or it is what I
meant, I mean.

Look, simply put, it's a chapter called 'The Next
Chapter' and it's a very clever device in a book
to do that. It's only because some of you are a bit
slow, that I'm having to explain to you what it
means. A lot of writers wouldn't do that you know.
They'd just take it for granted that you had
some intelligence. I'm not like that, I believe in
helping people less fortunate than me.

When I got home from school on whatever day this
was, I was just about to change into my playing

out clothes, when I heard Father's voice speaking
as he spoke to me from the next room.

"Come into the drawing room, there's a good
fellow", my ears heard. Which surprised me
greatly, because I didn't know we had a drawing
room.

Still like Bear Grylls, I followed the trail
of his voice. Or I should say, like Bear Grills
Granddad, because Bear Grills wasn't born yet
when this happened.

So, having cleared that up, I found myself in
what I called 'the front room' but father called,
'the drawing room', for reasons best known to
himself, which I never asked him about for the
rest of his life. Perhaps he was delusional. I'm
not a psychiatrist. In fact I'm sorry I mentioned
it, because it's irrelevant and possibly this bit
will be cut out? I don't know. And anyway I prefer
the other one. The fat one. Who's name escapes me.
Ray someone?

Video Coronation Street

When I entered, father was standing by the
fireplace, his hands in his trouser pockets,
winding up his pocket watch, somehow. A furrowed
expression graced his troubled visage.

"You wanted to see me father?" I remarked.
Ray Mears. That's the one. That's who I was
talking about. ←——————————————

See !!!
Ray
Means
is
fatter
than
Bear
Grills

"You wanted to see me father?" I remarked again.

"Yes my boy. Pull up a chair".

I pulled up a chair and waited expectantly, for
the next thing to happen.

He took a deep breath in, blew a bit of it out and
continued with what he was saying before the
breathing.

"Arthur, there comes a time in every boy's life
when it's the time to become a man. This is that
time".

"What, half past four?" I enquired.

"No. I didn't mean the exact time. Like on the
clock. I meant a more general period of time".

I must have looked a little confused because
father went on.

"I mean time as a dimension in which events
can be ordered from the past through the
present into the future. And also the measure of

durations of events and the intervals between them. Like it says on wickerpedia. More that sort of thing".

I nodded, slightly puzzled in truth, as I watched a fly, relentlessly circling the paisley patterned lampshade. Auntie Irene loved that lampshade and would stare at it for hours, if you let her. What did father mean? Why was he talking like this? Had he been in the Red Lion all day again? I remember the last time…

I had been practicing scales on the pianola. Suddenly the door opened. Father took two steps into the room, put his hand on the top of the piano to steady himself and slid the length of it, knocking a George the Fifth coronation bowl off, which hit the cat, killing it outright. He then started to crawl up the stairs muttering, "I'm not drunk, it's shell shock. Don't tell your mother about 'Fluffy'. He then threw a sixpenny bit at me and still on his hands and knees disappeared up the stairs.

I was aroused from this reverie by my actual father actually talking to the actual me.

"Arthur are you listening?" he injected.

Might sound like a drug addict?

I nodded. I hadn't the heart to tell him I was actually writing a book at the moment so couldn't give him my full attention.

"How old are you my boy", he interrogated me.

"Frankly I can't really remember Father, and I wish you hadn't asked me that." I replied. Let's say I was five. We don't want to fall out over a year or two.

Five father, said I.

"If you want me to hear your answer you've got to put it in inverted commas", he informed me.

He was right of course. If you're doing a book and you don't use them you can't tell when people are speaking. How could I have been so stupid!

Father suddenly went quiet and stared at the floor. It was almost as though someone had switched him off and it's partly because I've lost my thread and it might be time to go to the bookies anyway. Try my daily 'Patent'. Each way. Six crossed doubles, three trebles and an accumulator. if you get one of those up you're laughing.

[45]

Stamp

CHAPTER 8 AGAIN

THE NEXT CHAPTER AGAIN

I'll never forget that moment when father broke
the news to me. It's burned into my memory like a
cow being branded in a 'Western'. In fact whenever
I smell burning leather I'm right back there
in that drawing room, a small, approximately
five year old, wide eyed boy, with a lifetime of
triumphs and awards ahead of him.

As I intimated before I went to the bookies in
the last previous chapter, 'The Next Chapter' (the
name of the chapter. Not 'the next chapter', and
frankly I wish I'd never started with that) he
had called me into the drawing room to tell me
some news. The news was that he he and mother
had decided to take me out of school and take me
on the road with them. Educating and tutoring me
themselves. At first Mother was against the idea.
See how in the next chapter she comes round to
it.

CHAPTER 9

A STAR ID BORN

Chapter eight might not be long enough?

Well whether it is or not, at first Mother
tried to talk me out of following her into the
profession. "It's such a hard life, my darling",
she said, a favourite way of hers to talk to
people.

"So very few people make it in the 'profession'.
And you have such a fine mind Arthur, that I
really think that you could one day be the next
Lord Mayor of London. You've got to be better
than Boris Johnson is. Who in my opinion has got
something wrong with him and gets on my nerves
with his stupid hair and if I ever found myself
next to him with a pair of scissors I'd cut his
bloody fringe off", she mused, possessed almost
with a second sight.

But I wouldn't listen. I was four years old with
everything ahead of me. What cared I of the

affairs of state? What cared I for the trappings of high office? What cared I for another one I'll *find out what the other on is* think of after? Finally, seeing I could not be shifted in my resolve, she gave in and ceded to my request.

We put a new act together and it featured myself dressed as a baby in a pram. Father played my father and Mother played my mother. It's genius was it's simplicity.

The act was this. Mother would push me onstage, as though we were walking in the park. Father would be drunk and he and Mother would have a row. She'd storm off and he'd have to look after me. He kept falling asleep on a deck chair and I would keep getting out of the pram and kicking him up his behind, then getting back into the pram before he realised it was me.

And do you know it was even funnier than it sounds. After that first performance at The Newcastle Hippodrome, or somewhere similar, I'll never forget us sitting up all night waiting for the reviews to come in.

Stamps

We sat up all night waiting for the reviews
to come in and I'll never forget it. And here,
published in full, is the relevant bit of the
review which I'll never forget sitting up for,
all night, from the Newcastle Echo or something
similar, in 1945.

'THE PERFORMANCE OF THE BABY, PLAYED BY A CERTAIN
ARTHUR STRONG, WAS A NON STOP TOUR DE FRANCE. HIS
TIMING WAS IMPECCABLE AND THIS REVIEWER IS IN NO
DOUBT HE MIGHT GO ON TO BE AS BIG AS SOMEONE LIKE
MICHAEL MACINTYRE IN THE FUTURE'.

"A not stop tour de France!' it said! I couldn't
believe it. And at that time I didn't even have a
bike of my own. That a reviewer thought that I
was capable of winning the Tour de Force without
even having a bike, meant so much to me.

Of course, the Michael Macintyre of today,
hadn't been born yet. And anyway, if you read it
properly I said 'Someone LIKE him.' It's just pure
coincidence. And use of that name is for purely
illustrative purposes only.

Frankly I couldn't believe what I was reading.
The thought that someone thought that one day

I could be like someone like Michael MacKintyre,
was beyond the comprehension of a five year old.
In fact I'm still having trouble with it, and I
might have another go at that after Eggheads.

The Eggheads wo.
its fixed!

'A GIRL NAMED DORIS'

A WHODUNNIT?

By Count Arthur Strong.

'Apart from her cruel mouth, she was the kind
of dame that had all the curves in all the right
places. Blonde, tall, with to die for, deep blue
get yourself up to bed now eyes. The kind that
sucked you right in. In spite of everything I
felt kinda sorry for her.

I lit two cigarettes in my mouth at once and
handed one of them to her. Silently she took
it and had a puff, inhaling deeply. The smoke
caressed the inside of her lungs, satisfying
her need for nicotine. "So tell me what you know
about Moose Murphy", I uttered. She looked up at
the ceiling, silently rolling both of her eyes
of hers, inhaling deeply on her cigarette, as
though her life depended on it.

"Listen lady, this ain't no kindergarten", I
snapped losing my patience with her.

I took my cigarette case out of my inside pocket

[51]

and angrily opened it, lighting an cigarette from the other cigarette I already had on the go. I think they call it 'chain smoking'. I could see I'd upset her, and for the second time on this page, I felt kinda sorry for her.

Without speaking I crossed to the filing cabinet. I slid open the drawer and pulled out a bottle of White Horse. I poured two glasses out and drank them both. It had been a long night. I inhaled very deeply on my one or two cigarettes I'd lit, momentarily loosing count. Then I sat down on the chair. But not the way you normally do, I sat on it backwards, like they do in films. I pushed my trilby with the finger of the one next to my index finger of my left hand, so it tilted back on my head, and let out a sigh that seemed to go on forever. Finally I looked at her and with a half smile on half my face, I forget which half, I poured another glass and pushed it towards her. She took it and drank from it hungrily.

"Why are you half smiling at me?", she said.

"I'm sorry I behaved like a louse just then" I intoned, ignoring her question, like men do to women. She smiled a half smile all of her own, back at me.

"Touche", I uttered.

"You know, I can't quite work you out" she said, ruefully.

'Join the club lady' I wisecrapped.

Do you know, I don't think I've ever been as happy before for a long time. Sitting on that chair backwards, wisecrapping, blowing our smoke out at each other and drinking our White Horses'es. For a second I almost forgot myself and started singing 'The River Of No Return', my favourite Robert Mitchum film, but I knew somewhere deep down inside, call it a hump if you like, I just knew that, that door would open and someone would let the outside in. Suddenly, the door opened, just like I'd prophesied, and from the outside, a head poked it's head round the corner.

"Better come quick Chief", the poked head said, "We've had another anomanous telephone call".

"How do you know it was another one, if it was

anonamous?" I quipped faster than an express
train. I turned to Doris, "It looks like I'm
going to have to take a ten four. Stay where you
are", I uttered.

"Sure, I ain't got no plans" She spat back at
me. Like next doors cat.

"Swell. I'll see you around, in a bit."

Then I turned to the man who's head it was and
said,

"I want to know if she as much as breathes". And
without so much as a backward glance I left the
room behind me. Returning only to get my hat.
Then I left the room behind me again, properly.

As I drove at speed in the precinct squad car, I
ran over in my mind again and again, that time
Doris and I had met. It was etched in my mind,
like a cut glass is etched at the factory. I
could remember it like it was tomorrow. August
the 12th. It was kinda raining. The kinda rain
that kinda wet's you all over if you're not
careful, or have an umbrella. I was working
the east side when I got a call saying the
neighbourhoods hood's were in the hood, having

a meet, so I thought I'd show my face and throw them a frightener, see if I could pick any leads up up.

When I rounded the corner of east and forty second, I saw the four of them, standing there. Smelly Joe, Dip the Stick, Jones the Post and Moose Murphy himself. We nodded our heads at each other. I took out my packet of cigarettes out, lit five in my mouth at once and gave each of them, one each between them. Then I lit another five for myself. Moose looked up at me and said, "You know, you ought to quit".

I said, "Yes. But what you've forgot Moose is, when this book is set they didn't know smoking was bad for you because I've just researched that up in a Women's Own. So come back in another twenty years".

Just then, the door opened and we all looked to see what it was. It was the door opening, and through it came Doris.

Ah Doris. She walked over swinging her hips of hers, like a pendulum does in any clock that might have one. We all lit a cigarette for her

and waited breathless. She surveyed the scene
for what seemed an eternity, before she elected
to choose mine. Moose glowered at me.

"Can I get you a cocktail" I uttered to her, the
breath catching in my throat as I was uttering.

"I'll have something long and cool", she
retorted.

"Just like you", I retorted myself.

"Nice retorting", added Moose Murphy enviously.

"There's plenty more where that came from",
I retorted once more, yet again confirming my
superiority at retortering . . .

Moose didn't take the bait this time. He knew
I was a better retorter than him, and he could
only ever come a poor second at retorting, when
I was in the room.

CHAPTER ?

MY FRIENDS IN THE NORTH

SO SUCCESSFUL WAS OUR ACT THAT . . . OH FOR CRYING
OUT LOUD! THE THING'S STUCK ON THAT DOES CAPITALS.
THE KEY. WHY WON'T THAT COME OFF? I'M GOING TO HAVE
TO GO AND GET A HAMMER NOW OR SOMETHING BECAUSE
OF THIS. AND THIS IS EATING INTO MY WRITING TIME
AS WELL!!! REMEMBER THAT WHEN YOU'RE SCREAMING
AT ME FOR THE BOOK. I DON'T KNOW WHY I CAN'T HAVE
A DECENT TYPEWRITER? YOU WOULDN'T GIVE ONE LIKE
THIS TO JILLY COOPER WOULD YOU? OR ALAN TITSMARSH.
THEY'D BE LAUGHING THEIR HEADS OFF IF THEY SAW
WHAT I HAVE TO WRITE ON. I SHOULD HAVE A BIT MORE
MONEY UPFRONT FOR UNFORESEEN CIRCUMSTANCES LIKE
THIS IS. THAT PITTANCE YOU GAVE ME'S LONG GOne.
Oh that's better. It was the other key. Not that
one. THAT ONE. TThey shouldn't put them so close
together. It's bad design is that.

ScrUB all this. I'll start agaiN.

Stupid stupid typewriter !!!

[57]

CHAPTER 4

A BOOK, A BOOK, MY KINGDOM FOR A BOOK!

So succcessful had our act become that we
were asked to stay on in Newcastle for an
unprecedented five week run. Dad and Mam, or
whatever I call them now, rented a two up, two
down, one round the corner, Victorian terrace
house with an outside lavatory.

For some reason the Victorians thought having
a toilet in the house was unhygienic, the idiots.
Preferring to urinate in a basin they kept under
the bed. Then some poor sod like me had to carry
the bloody thing to the outside toilet, without
spilling it, whatever the weather. Where's the
sense in that. It's what the ergonomists call,
'double handling' that.

'We are not Amused'. You can say that again.

I tried to fit in with the local children, but
frankly they resented me because of my success
and top hat. Let's face it, I wasn't like them. I

wore the aforementioned top hat, blew my nose on
a monogrammed handkerchief and was well spoken
when I spoke. They wore holy balaclavas, (one's
with holes in. Not religious), used their sleeve
arms to wipe on and couldn't really speak, to
speak of. Instead choosing to make a series of
almost musical, grunting noises, which I came
to understand is what they call 'Geordie'. It's a
bit like what they call speech in Liverpool but
not quite as bad. Do you know I can't understand
a single word that, that John Bishop says. He
said something last night that was like "Weeeeee
youugizzgozgazznnooocumonnwweeellgahhkgahhk
gahhk" It's like he's choking or something. I
wonder how many times people have jumped up and
tried to give him the kiss of life during his act,
or the Heiniken Manouverment? If you can call
it an act? It's just a lazy way of speaking. It's
like Welsh. That advert for the Postcode Lottery.
I can't understand what him in the Welsh rugby
shirt's saying in that. My numbers could have
come up and I wouldn't have a clue. Maybe that's
why they're doing it? Get announcers that don't
speak properly to do it and no one will ever
know they've won. Then someone's pocketing the

money. They must think we were born the day before yesterday that lot.

That's what they did in the war. The BBBC got Wilfred Pickles to read the news, because they thought the Germans wouldn't understand his dialect. Nobody else could neither. For five years no one knew what the news was.

Despite my celebrity status I was, is, and always have been, a shy, humble and sensitive person, *and* when I'm away from the cameras, or an audience, *magnanimo* or a bus stop, and unbelievable though it may sound to you about someone like me, I found it difficult to make friends with my peers. I found *pier* I had so little in common with them. There was the language barrier for a start as I outlined previous and for another thing, I just couldn't bring myself to eat coal, like everybody else did up there. It wasn't so much the taste, in fact him that sells the Big Issue says it's actually good for you, it was the smell of it. So all these things put together made me feel a little bit ostriched by the people up there.

I was working every night of course at the theatre, so I decided that during the day I would

put all my energies into self educating myself.
Little did I know just what a momentous decision
that decision was, I've just told you about, was. *too many* *was is*

Through my life, the fact that I'm well educated
has opened doors for me, quite literally, almost.
Because of my education, I have walked with
paupers and Lord Mayors's in equal measure. And
I have always treated everybody as equal. From
the dirtiest person you cross the road to avoid
that's asking for money, to Dukes and Duchesses's,
all are equal in my eyes, more or less. And that's
all down to me being educated.

Sometimes people ask me what was the most
important facet, the most important part of my
life's journey, and I always tell them, without
hesitation, it was being able to swallow a sword
and my education. And having my bunions done. *lose*
And learning to drive . . . I might rethink this *bunions*
bit. There 's a bigger list than I thought there
was once you get going on it.

I'd always been an avid reader. Magazines,
newspapers, the back of the Sugar Puffs packet
- anything with letters in it formed into words
and then sentences, paragraphs, chapters and
ultimately books.

In fact it was said in the family, that when I was born I came out of Mother with a book in my hand. I don't know whether that's true or not, or if it was what they call apocraphal. I have no memory of it. So I can not rule it in or rule it out. If it was true, I'd like to know how the book got up there? And what book it was? Probably a 'Dicken's' knowing the young me as I did and do.

I devoured the works of Charles Dickens and would pour over them under the eiderdown, with a only a tin of sardines and box of matches to illuminate the pages, long after I was susposed to be asleep. My favourite one of his, was 'Alice in Wonderland' and if I read it once, I read it a hundred times. Or fifty then.

Funnily enough, one of my favourite places to read has always been on the toilet. It's got nothing to do with the usual use of the facilities, I hasten to add. It's just for some reason I always feel like reading in there, once I get sat down. I'll often end up reading the back of a bottle of shampoo or something, if I'm taken short and don't have time to pick a book up on the way in. Fortunately that doesn't happen as

toilet pa,
potatoes
Liver
Mars ba

often as it used to, now I'm on the other pills. Anyway that's how avid a reader I am.

I came up with a marvellous idea for breaking the ice with the Geordie coal children. I decided I would perform a benefit show for them, to raise awareness for their plight, just like they do on Children In Need. In fact you could say, because of this, it was me and not Terry Wogan that invented and created Children in Need. A fact that everyone has conveniently seemed to forget. Not that I believe you should go round blowing your own trumpet up yourself, like he does.

I mean I've been involved in charity work for longer than I can shake a stick at. In fact I was at a charity gala the other night, for my favourite charity which I'm a figurehead for, 'Stop The Dolphins'. No it wasn't that. Not 'Stop the Dolphins'. 'Stop the Orphans'. No. It wasn't that either. You can't stop orphans can you? The one where she's stood outside the chemists with her leg in a calliper. 'Doctor Barnum's Houses'. That's it. You buy houses for them. Off Doctor Barnum. And I'm a figurehead for that. Oh yes I'm a great giver backerer. Do you know I think I'm only

truly happy when I'm surrounded by those less
fortunate than myself.

Over the years, I've raised so much for so many,
with so little, that people affectionately refer
to me as the Jack the Ripper of the charity
world. Which is lovely of them, to do that. Not
Jack the Ripper! Robin Hood. (You'll check all this
won't you? In case I've done that before. Jack the
Ripper was a murderer I think).

Jack the Ripper — Whitechapel
Robin Hood — Sherwood
               Monsest.
Little John.
Will Scarlet.
Friar Tuck,
Maid Marion.
Alan a Dale.
Launcelot.
Little John.
cheese
[64]
toilet paper

CHAPTER

OLD FRIENDS

The wonderful thing about the Variety Theatre
in those days was, being on a circuit, the acts
were constantly changing. Like bags of luggage
on an airport carousel do, and there was always
the opportunity to meet old friends. I say that
because the next bit after this line is about
just that, and this has been a preamble into
it. It's a device we writers use for such things
as this. And I want you to feel free to take
all these tips I'm giving you. for only a small
voluntary contribution, which you must let your
conscience dictate.

Possibly a pound?

It was a damp Tuesday afternoon. The north
eastern wind was gusting, blowing a leaf across
the cobbled Newcastle streets. A sentence that
perhaps a young Catherine Cookson might have
dreamed about writing in one of her books.
Possibly one about a defrocked vicar having an
illegitimate child that the squire's son falls in

love with, then he gets killed in the war and she realises she's having his baby, then she end's up marrying the squire to cover that up and when he finds out he throws her out and she's found a week later on the roadside by some travellers, and she has the baby and dies, so they take the baby with them and when it grows up, it comes back to claim it's inheritance from the squire, who's never got over it and welcomes it back with open arms. And I'd be good as the squire in that, if they made that into a film. Because I've been told that I have authority.

Squire Anthur Squir Str

A flat capped man, coat muffled up against the elements, struggles against the wind as he crosses the road and enters the stage door of the theatre, just in to time for the afternoon matinee. Once he'd unmuffled himself, I could see that it was none other than our old friend Bendy Bob from Doncaster! From the contortionist act my mother used to be in. It was wonderful to meet an old friend again. In fact it was just like meeting an old friend. Again. And after we all slapped each other on our backs and said our hello's, Bob told us that after mother had left the act, the rest of them all went their separate

ways. Jerky John was arrested for burglary,
Elastic Eileen became a nun and Bob went solo,
apart from another person in his act, who's name
escapes me.

What Bob's act was is

What Bob's act is was

What Bob's act was was

What Bob's act is, is ⟵   *I don't know which ones right now.*

he used to come onstage and there'd be a suitcase
in the middle of it, he'd then squash himself into
it and the other one of the solo act, who's name
escapes me, would come and carry it off.

And do you know, if Bob was short of money he'd
sometimes stay in the suitcase after the show
and the other one, who's name escapes me, would
carry it on the train. He saved himself a fortune
in travelling expenses. He did it for years that.
And he was doing alright until the Great Train
Robbery. He was never heard of again. Imagine the
look on Ronald Biggs'is face when he opened that
suitcase, and Bendy Bob fell out. He thought he'd

Stamps

stolen a suitcase full of letters from the post office. Not a Doncaster based contortionist with dislocated arms and legs.

Anyway it was lovely to see Bob before he went missing and I never saw him again.

More waste

CHAPTER

THE PAGES OF MY JOURNAL

One of the things that's has been a useful tool
to me in the writing of this wonderful memoir,
are my scrupulously dated and detailed diaries
I've always kept since I was a small boy child.
And I just thought when I was having my egg
that it would be marvellous for you to see some
excerpts from them in their true form. So what
I've done is just delved into them at random and
her follows some salient and pertinent entries.

look what salient means up.

Wednesday, January 7th 1963.
Great news! England have just won the World Cup
at football with goals by Nobbly Stiles and Alf
Ramsey. Which is marvellous news. Particularly
for people that like football. Because there are
so many idiots out on the street celebrating, I'm
almost late to arrive at the Adelphi Theatre for
my show tonight. When I do get to my dressing
room, my understudy, a spotty youth named Albert
Finney, who's name escapes me, is already in his

underpants with one leg in my show trousers. Would he be so fast to jump into my grave, I mentally make one of those mental notes of. He's a strange young man is Finney. He has the look to me of someone who might put on a lot of weight and not be very good in 'Skyfall' sometime in the future. With me barely being able to understand what he is saying in it, in parts. I didn't know it was him at first. I thought who's that dirty old sod? Where've they got him from? In fact when he came on I nearly got up and left. I would have done if I hadn't been at home watching a VD of it. Oh he's really let himself go. Don't get me wrong I've seen him be good in things. Mind you he's not really done anything of note since 'Some Mother's Do Have Them' has he? But credit where credit's due, he was good in that, doing his woopsies for Betty all over the carpet.

Anyway our show is a musical version of Bridge Up The River Kwai, in which I'm obviously playing the lead role, made famous by the Alex Guinness of the same name. And actually every one I know says I should have done the film instead of him. Though you'll not hear me saying that because I'm magnanimous about it.

1·9

3·9

·9

——

6·9

2

she owes me

£6·97

Left the theatre at 10.25 to have dinner with the late Max Bygraves and Jimmy Clitheroe, who was on time.

He may have been on time, but Jimmy's in a foul mood. First he wants ice cream with his potatoes. Then he messes his trousers and won't stop crying. And all night long he's blowing on a little plastic trumpet. I tell you I wouldn't have come if it wasn't his turn to pay. After the pudding, (semolina), I make my excuses and leave. Fall asleep on the 31 again, awaken at terminus. Get home half past three. Straight to bed, to sleep perchance to dream.

Saturday, August 7th 1980.
An audition for 'The Sound of Music', by Rogers and Hammerhead. For a tour of sports halls I think, or something. Although no one's said, I'm obviously up for the Christopher Plummel part in it. And I have to say they were terribly rude people I saw. Terribly rude. The one that had his glasses on a chain round his neck, stopped me halfway through the song I was singing. When I said, "What have you stopped me for? I was just getting to a good bit."

He said, "You don't seem to know what the name of the song you're singing's called. It's called Eidelweiss".

I said "Oh no it is not!" I said, "Listen I don't know what version of the film you've seen, but I've got a video of it when they did it on 'Russ Abbot's Madhouse' and it's definitely 'Idleswine' they're singing in that. I've done my scrupulous research I'm famous for on it". I said, "I think you'll find it's a song about a lazy member of the Hitler Youth". That shut him up.

Yes and I said, "Hey and I'll tell you something else you never hear them saying about the Sound of Mucus. She makes those children - seven of them - she makes them clothes out of a big pair of curtains, fifteen foot high, as if that's a cheap way of doing it. Have you seen how much curtaining is? It's a fool's economy that is. And there's a war on, the blackout. Light flooding out of the window through all the dress shaped holes she's cut. All the Gestapo would have to do is to match the clothes against the holes and bingo! You're in a concentration camp. It's a wonder we ever won the war, with Julie Andrews on our side. Absolute madness.

[72]

Then I offered to do 'Sixteen going on Seventeen?', but they didn't want a second song. Probably 'When I'm 64?' because 'Idlesod' couldn't be bettered.

December 12th 1980

No post this morning. Get batteries. Still nothing from the Sound of Mucus people. If I've not heard by Friday I'll give them a call. They're probably trying to make me sweat because I put them straight on a couple of things. Which I think is quite pathetic. They want to grow up if you ask me, be more mature about it.

Had a big row with her at the post office. Putting the stamps up again. I said to her, "Can you explain to me how the post office can justify putting the Penny Black up year on year until we're where where we are today? It's scandalous!"

Anyway I didn't have time to stand around because I had to get home to do my horrorscopes for the church magazine.

Do you know, I'd forgotten I did Horrorscopes in the 80's.

I tell you what I'll do, as a bonus here, on the

next page everybody, are tomorrows stars. At no
extra charge, unless you feel moved to offer
me something for it? What about that then? You
wouldn't get Charles Dickens doing horrorscopes
in the middle of one of his books would you. He's
missed a trick there.

TOMORROWS STARS

BY

COUNT ARTHUR STRONG

Aries: The sign of the ram.
A letter brings you news about a loved one. In
the afternoon your telephone may stop working.
The steering will fail on your car. Heed my
warning.

Gemini: The sign of the twins.
For most Gemini's things come in two's, for obvious
reasons, which could be deemed a bit greedy, if it
was say, two dinners. Just remember that and mind
your manners. I always thought it'd be nice for
me to have a twin brother.

Carpricorn: The sign of the . . . I don't know what
it is? Looks like another ram but there can't be
two rams can there? It's possibly a goat. We'll
call it a goat for now.
The sign of the goat. Look out for a wolf in

sheep's clothing bearing gifts. Eat some raw
garlic and keep all you windows shut. Unless
you're outdoors, obviously.

Serpico: The sign of the Lobster.
Not to be confused with the film, Serpico, which I
enjoyed and was on last night. Serpicorean's?, are
by nature shy and retiring. So just keep doing
what you're doing and stay out of our way.

Virgo: The sign of a woman holding a plant.
I once knew a virgo who was round the twist and
I've never really liked them as a consequence.
Read a book.

Leo: The sign of the Lion.
The lion is the king of the jungle and like the
lion, you are refined and have great charisma,
are a natural entertainer and much loved by all.
You deserve to be, you've worked hard to get where
I am. Congratulations!

Aquarius: The water ewer holderer.
You're too trusting. If you were more suspicious
of people and not so stupid, you might have made

something of yourself Ann. Come back tomorrow
and I'll do your tarot cards. Lucky colour -
turquoise.

Cancer: The sign of Crabs.
The crabs can be nasty, so you want to guard
against that. And they can give you a nasty
nip, if you're not careful, like ferrets. I like
them with a bit of mayonnaise and some salt on
them in a sandwich. Crabs I mean. Not ferrets. I
wouldn't eat a ferret. Unless it was me or it. A
house move might be on the cards.
Favourite colour - Mangenta

Libra: The weighing scales of justice.
Librarians tend to make good Judges or Justices
of the peace's. So if you're not one already, it
sounds like a career change is in the stars at
the end of the rainbow. Get a book on it and stop
bothering me.
Favourite thing - the seed drill.

Sagittarious: The horse with a man's front. Well
I'm saying 'Man's front' I've never been sure how
far down it goes, if you get my drift. They always

Stamps

obscure that bit out whenever I've seen one in drawings or in a film. So I can honestly say, hand on heart, that I have no idea how you lot go about your 'ablutions' shall we call it? You must just hope for the best in the cubicle. Good luck with it all! What I do know is that a centaur's lucky favourite colour might be green.

Scorpio: The sign of the lobster. (Although it just looks like a crab).
Not to be confused with the film 'Scorpio' of the same name. Famous 'Scorpio-reans' include Al Pacino from one of my favourite films, coincidentally also called 'Scorpio'. Hoo ha! And that's typical of you lot. Clear as mud. Favourite Celebrity, Arthur Askey.

This level of waste is tolerab

Rhubarb Wine Recipe

Ingredients

10 to 12 cups thinly sliced rhubarb

1 4-inch cinnamon stick (optional)

7 cups granulated sugar

2 campden tablets

1 tsp. nutrients

1/2 tsp. pectic enzyme

1 pkg. wine yeast

1 gallon water

Directions

Put the water into the primary fermentor.

Add the pectic enzyme and crushed campden tablet. Stir well.

Add the rhubarb and let mixture sit for two days, stirring regularly.

Strain, but DO NOT squeeze.

Dissolve the sugar and the nutrients in the liquid. Check specific gravity. It should be between 1.100 and 1.110.

Add yeast and mix in well. Cover the primary fermentor and let sit overnight.

Siphon into secondary fermentor, add cinnamon (if desired), and attach airlock.

For a dry wine: Rack in three weeks and return to secondary fermentor. Rack again in three months, and every three month until one year old. Bottle.

For a sweet wine: Rack at three weeks. Add 1/2 cup sugar dissolved in 1 cup of wine. Stir in gently, and place back into the secondary fermentor. Repeat this process every six weeks until fermentation does not restart with the addition of sugar. Rack every three months until one year old. Bottle.

*Note: This Rhubarb Wine will taste the very best if you can refrain from drinking it for a year and a half from the date it was started.

CHAPTER 9

THE END OF THE WAR

It was 1945 when it happened. I remember I was fast
asleep in bed, when I was awoken up by a cacophony
of loud noises from outside my window pane.

At first I couldn't believe what I was hearing.
I thought I must be dreaming it, and then I
thought what if I'm dreaming thinking I thought
I was dreaming it? And then I remembered I'd been
dreaming about a big cat, wearing a dress, that
was hitting me with a stick because I wouldn't
eat my soup. I didn't know what to do, where to
turn, what to say. Or who to say it to, if I knew
what to say or do or where to turn.

Suddenly I was wrested out of this conundrum
by what sounded like a military band playing. I
arose out of bed and crossed sensitively to the
olive green curtains, unceremoniously flinging
them aside in my haste to look out of the window.
Obviously we didn't know the curtains were olive
green then. No one knew what an olive was in

1940's England. In fact I didn't have an olive
until 1974. And when I did I wished I hadn't. Even
now I will ask for a bowl to spit them into if
someone puts them in a meal at a restaurant. I
had to put some in a plant pot once when I was
at a Variety Club of Great Britain do for David
Berglass. I think it was David Berglass? He is an
illusionist, so it might not have been him. *How would
1) find
that
out?*

And I can't abide parmesan neither. It smells like
sick. I had some in a sandwich once once and it
just tastes like candle wax, but not as nice. *Phone up
the
internet?*

Outside I could see that what I'd thought was a
brass band playing, was a brass band playing.
And people were marching behind it shouting. 'It's
the end of the war! It's the end of the war!' What
on earth did they mean? I pondered to myself,,
trying to make some sense of the scene being
acted out before my eyes of mine.

Once I'd collected myself, because it would
have been stupid to go downstairs without me, I
rushed downstairs. Mother and father were on the
doorstep with the door ajar, their eyes shining
with tears of joy in their eyes. "It's over old
fellow. It's over!" ejaculated father.

It was then I realised! It was over! It was over!

"What's over?" I said puzzled.

"Why, my boy, the second world war of course".

"Does that mean you won't have to limp anymore father" I intoned. Father dropped his head back and laughed like an infectious hyena. Mother joined in and soon they'd infected the whole street. We must have looked quite a sight. But we didn't care, the war was over! And we'd survived it.

CHAPTER 14

BACK TO NORMAL

With the war over, things were slowly getting
back to normal. The news had filtered through
to us from Germany that Adolph Hitler had
killed himself to death in a bunker. What he was
doing in there I guess we'll never know. Perhaps
he fell in whilst trying to fill the scuttle?
Reaching out desperately for the last bit of coal
in those just post war days.

Perhaps a small kitten had got trapped in there
and was mewing, I reasoned. Hitler might have
gone to see what the noise was, tripped over his
own jack boots and Bob's your uncle.

It was just a senseless accident and ironic that
it should happen just when peace broke out.
To think he'd got all the way through the war,
only to die, possibly rescuing a cat. Mother had
always told me to stay out of our coal bunker.
And the fact that I'm still here today attests
to the astuteness of her good advice. God bless

her for that. If you'd have been Hitler's mother,
mother, he may well be here today. A sobering
thought.

Although we were still proving popular on the
variety circuit, Mother wanted to move back to
London, so move back to London we did. Stopping
off in Doncaster to say a quick farewell to
Auntie Aunty Irene, who said she didn't know who
we were and wouldn't let us back into the house.

I've always had a soft spot for Doncaster
because of my time spent there during the war
and consider it my second home. Well third home
I should say. I do have a half share in a beach
hut in Kilnsea with my butcher and I'm able
to stay there, unmolested, every third week in
November. When it's not burnt down. Which wasn't
my fault. And just like Patric Moore I've had many
lovely nights there, sat in a deck chair with my
binoculars out, looking for the Aurora Boreolis.

After the celebrations of VD Day had died down
it became clear that things would be hard for
some time yet. We still had rationing to contend
with and the pig had gone missing, like Shergar,
presumed eaten by person or persons unknown.

tea ba

That's the **pig** I mean. Not Shergar. That is a mystery.

My theory is that someone took it stuck an onion in it's mouth and cooked it up with some apple sauce. The **pig** I mean again. Not Shergar. I wish I hadn't mentioned bloody Shergar. It's just confusing. I personally think that whoever took it must have been someone known to it.

Shergar I mean not the **pig**!

Of course we were still growing our own vegetables, which I'm not going to list again. I've done it once. If you're that bothered look for the page and read it again. And while we're on vegetables, I went out to get some sausages last night from Londis because John said they had some on offer, and when I got home with them and cooked them up, I thought there was something wrong, so I got the packet out of the bin and they were all made of vegetables. There was no meat in them at all. They were Paul McCartney's ones. From the pop group. So I had to go out again, with my knees, and get some <u>proper</u> sausages. And then I had the Paul McCartney sausages with those sausages as vegetables.

Which looked a bit odd because all I had on the plate in the end was what looked like about fifty sausages. Mind you it's a good use for a vegetable sausage is that, having it with your meat. I'm still going to try and get my money back though. Trades Description Act. You can't call it a sausage unless there's a good about 6 to 8% meat in there. I'm going to send John Lennon a letter about that.

This one!
(not the other one

CHAPTER 15

WHAT'S THAT ALL ABOUT

Mother wanted me to go back to school and for
a time I did. But frankly I was so far ahead
of everybody, even the teachers that it was
pointless. I would just sit there everyday
waiting fro them all to catch up. Eventually
they saw sens and asked me to leave, because I   *sense*
was so brainy. In fact, I was the top percentile
in the school.

I've always had a natural aptitude for
everything and in 1980 something I was paid the
highest accolade possible and made and Honarary
Thesis or something, of Oxford University and
asked to address the famous Oxford Union. I
spoke without notes for what someone later told
me 'Seemed like an age', and I reproduce for you
after this sentence, what a stenographer wrote
down verbatim, just after I'd uttered each word.

COUNT ARTHUR STRONG

FULL TRANSCRIPT OF ADDRESS TO OXFORD UNION

1980 SOMETHING

SUBJECT:

CREATIONALISM V NATURALISM

"Nice to be here. At my age it's nice to be
anywhere. Go on, be honest.

In the beginning God said, 'Let there be light',
and there was light, radiant and bright. God
called the light day. Just like we do and the
darkness he called night. Again which is just
what we call it. So so far, Oxford University, he's
only calling things what we already know they
are. And that we call a trend.

On the second day God created Adam and Eve from
some spare ribs. I don't know where he got those
from. No one thought to ask. Adam and Eve, naked
as the day they were born walked hand in hand
through the Garden of Eden. They nibbled on one
delicious fruit after another. Apples, oranges,
pears, nectarines and tangerines are just some
examples of what fruit is.

[88]

When I was researching up on the Garden of
Eden, I asked my greengrocer, Allan Clifford, who
drinks in the 'Woodpecker', for a ball park number
of just how many fruits there would have been
in those days, and he said did Alan that there
would have to be somewhere in the region of
between fifty different ones. And that's coming
from an expert in the field, who's had his own
fruit shop established 1963.

Now I don't know if you believe any of that, what
I've just said to you from the 'Good Book'. Because
there are people who come down on the other side
of the tent. And these people we call the Natural
Selection people. And perhaps the most famous of
them was Charles Dance the explorer who sailed
to the north pole on HMS . . . It was named after
a dog? Not labrador . . . It's got longer ears
than a labrador . . . Oh we'll say it was a Basset
Hound. It's not that but it's near enough. Now
I've read his book, 'The Oranges of the Species',
scrupulously from cover to cover, you would
expect no less of me, and I think I've found it's
'Achilles Heel' if you will.

According to him we all come from the gorillas.

[89]

Fair enough. So far so good Charles Dance, well
done you. But the question he never answers is,
A) Who made the gorillas? And B) How come there
are still gorillas today if they've all turned
into us? You can't have it both ways. It's like
Charlton Heston. One minute he's Moses, the Ten
Commandments. The next minute he's talking to a
gorilla! And it's talking back, riding round on a
horse with a rifle in his hand. *Shergar ?*

Now it's not my job to tell you what to think
about Charles Dance and his naturism. I simply
present you with the facts. If they want to
play tennis in the nude, or tiddley winks, or
fry eggs in the nude, that's their business.
As long as they don't start imposing their
beliefs and letting it all hang out around us.
Though frankly I wouldn't go near hot fat in my
underpants, let alone in the 'altogether'. That's
just an accident waiting to happen. And you'll
find a lot of the women that do it are quite fat.
You have a look next time there's a programme on.

So Oxford University, did we come from the
gorillas as Charles Dance advocates. Or were we
made by God as the Archbishop of Canterbury and

Cliff Richards would have us believe? The choice ladies and gentlemen of the jury is yours. Thank you for listening to what I spake. You've been a lovely audience, I've been Count Arthur Strong."

* * * * *

Apart from all my drink I never got paid for that, you know. In fact it wasn't about the money, I did it to give something back. Although it wouldn't have hurt them to pay me a bit would it? I mean they're susposed to have a bit of money aren't they Oxford? Morse drove a Jaguar Mk2 didn't he?

Hey and I'll tell you what, they've never done a 'Time Team' on the garden of Eden have they? I might write into them about that. They'd find all sorts. Though it never says anything in the bible about what they had then does it? It just says they ate fruit really. That's not my idea of paradise. All the fruit you can eat. I'd want some proper tinned soup and a nice car. And I know they had snakes, because one bit Eve on the asp when she was having a bath of milk, but did they have any other animals there? Because that would be quite dangerous.

Anyway, whatever they had he's slipped up there, Tony Robinson. He's got his fingers in too many pies, that's what's up with him. He wants to pack the acting in and concentrate on the alchohology programmes. I couldn't understand what he was saying when he did the waiter in Fawlty Towers. Mr Faulty had to keep explaining to people he was from Spain. A bit of a cock up in the casting department if you ask me. Strangely enough I can understand him in 'Time Team', so I suppose he must have picked the language up. So fair play to him for that.

CHAPTER 28

I ARRIVE AT BUTLINS

I, Ishmael, was one of that crew; my shouts had gone up with
the rest; my oath had been welded with theirs; and stronger I
shouted, and more did I hammer and clinch my oath, because of
the dread in my soul. A wild, mystical, sympathetical feeling was
in me; Ahab's quenchless feud seemed mine. With greedy ears I
learned the history of that murderous monster against whom I
and all the others had taken our oaths of violence and revenge.

For some time past, though at intervals only, the unaccom-
panied, secluded White Whale had haunted those uncivilized
seas mostly frequented by the Sperm Whale fishermen. But not
all of them knew of his existence; a few of them, comparative-
ly, had knowingly seen him; while the number who as yet had
actually and knowingly given battle to him, was small indeed.
For, owing to the large number of whale-cruisers; the disorderly
way they were sprinkled over the entire watery circumference,
many of them adventurously pushing their quest along solitary
latitudes, so as seldom or never for a whole twelvemonth or more
on a stretch, to encounter a single news-telling sail of any sort;
the inordinate length of each separate voyage; the irregularity
of the times of sailing from home; all these, with other circumstances, direct and indirect, long obstructed the spread through
the whole world-wide whaling-fleet of the special individualiz-
ing tidings concerning Moby Dick. It was hardly to be doubted,
that several vessels reported to have encountered, at such or
such a time, or on such or such a meridian, a Sperm Whale of

uncommon magnitude and malignity, which whale, after doing great mischief to his assailants, has completely escaped them; to some minds it was not an unfair presumption, I say, that the whale in question must have been no other than Moby Dick. Yet as of late the Sperm Whale fishery had been marked by various and not unfrequent instances of great ferocity, cunning, and malice in the monster attacked; therefore it was, that those who by accident ignorantly gave battle to Moby Dick; such hunters, perhaps, for the most part, were content to ascribe the peculiar terror he bred, more, as it were, to the perils of the Sperm Whale fishery at large, than to the individual cause. In that way, mostly, the disastrous encounter between Ahab and the whale had hitherto been popularly regarded.

And as for those who, previously hearing of the White Whale, by chance caught sight of him; in the beginning of the thing they had every one of them, almost, as boldly and fearlessly lowered for him, as for any other whale of that species. But at length, such calamities did ensue in these assaults – not restricted to sprained wrists and ankles, broken limbs, or devouring amputations – but fatal to the last degree of fatality; those repeated disastrous repulses, all accumulating and piling their terrors upon Moby Dick; those things had gone far to shake the fortitude of many brave hunters, to whom the story of the White Whale had eventually come.

CHAPTER 20

HUGIE GREEN

'Opportunity Knocks' was the biggest television
show, on or off television, through the 1960's, and
in 1960 something I auditioned for it. I can still
remember how delighted Hughie Green was to see
me again. Having only that afternoon shouted at
him from across the street. I'm sure if he would
have remembered that, I would have been a shoe
in for the television stages.

By then I was playing a saw with a violin bow
for an act, and although someone had been on
the television rounds of Op Knocks doing it once
before, they hadn't cut themselves badly in the
auditions like I did. And I was fast making a
name for myself with this new take on playing a
saw. I had fourteen stitches in that cut, breaking
my record. In fact cutting one's self playing the
saw was such a natural hazard of the act, that I
actually wrote Roy Castle a letter to try and get
in the Guinness Book of Records. But he said that

there was no such record as cutting yourself
with a saw whilst playing 'Colonel Bogie'. Which
I think was the Guinness Book of Records' loss.
Still he sent me a nice signed picture did Roy. Of
himself and a trumpet. Him and that trumpet were
a real gentleman.

Mind you, it's changed a bit since then, the
Guinness Book. There's a record for everything
now. I was looking in one in the charity shop
and they've got a record for some idiot standing
for 60 seconds with 250 tarantulas on him.
Honestly, the things people will do for their
two minutes of fame! You wouldn't catch me
humiliating myself like that. And anyway the pet
shop near me said they couldn't get hold of 251
tarantulas.

I said, "Well thank you very much". I said, "Where
does that leave me now? You've just cost me a
world record!. Have you got lots of any other
animal?"

He said, "We've got a Llama".

I said, "I know! I know you've got a Llama. You
keep it out the back don't you? It's spat at

[96]

Stamp

anyone that's stupid enough to come up your back passage. Anyway, I'm not going to stand for sixty seconds with a Llama all over me. I'm not an idiot".

He said, "I've got four hamsters."

So I asked him to put them by for me for a day or two, until I'd had chance to go back to the Oxfam shop and seen if there are any records you can do with four hamsters.

Anyway, to cut a long story short, when I got back to Oxfam they'd only sold the bloody book hadn't they! It's like I'm destined not to get in that. I might just give it up and concentrate on my 'Who's Who' entry.

Micheal Caine

Marty Caine

Caine Mutiny

Caine and Abel?

Russel Caine?

Bamboo Caine

CHAPTER 21

PRESIDENT KENNEDY

It is said that everyone remembers where
President Kennedy was the night

CHAPTER 22

PRESIDENT KENNEDY

I'll never forget where President Kennedy was
the night I was

CHAPTER 23

PRESIDENT KENNEDY

People often say, 'If you can't remember President Kennedy, you weren't there the night he died

CHAPTER 24

PRESIDENT KENNEDY

Do you know how I remember where President
Kennedy was the night I

2 onions
Stamps

CHAPTER 25

PRESIDENT KENNEDY

How I remember when President Kennedy died is
because I know where he was

CHAPTER 26

PRESIDENT KENNEDY

When I was assassinated

Oh I've had enough of this, I'm going to write
about something else in the morning.

CHAPTER 18

WHERE TO NOW?

I'm late starting this, this morning so I'll have
a job on to do my words you want, because the
tape recorder I bought so I could start dictating
all this instead of thumping away on this
bloody thing until my fingers are stumps, was
malfunctioning. I've had to go all the way back
to Argos with it. And I'd done about half an hour
of solid dictatoring on it, or so I thought. About
the Royal Command Performance. And that's all
lost now. I'll have to make all that up again. The
second time's never as good if you have to make
things up twice. You won't believe the trouble I
had getting the bloody thing changed.

I said to the woman in there, "Listen I haven't
got time for malfunctioning machinery. I'm a very
important and busy writer and author".

She said, "What's wrong with it?".

"Listen to this", I said and I pressed the play
button. Then this woman's voice came on saying,

"I don't know what to say. Shall I say something about my new shoes? Well they're black patent, with a stiletto heel, Oh I sound just like your Auntie Lily on the tape recorder don't I?".

Then I switched it off and said to her, "What have you got to say about that?"

She looked at me like there was something wrong with me, then she ejaculated, "What's wrong with that? It sounds clear enough to me".

I said, "That's supposed to be a funny anecdote about Kenny Ball and his Jazzmen" That's what's wrong with that.

She said, "Look what's your complaint? There's people waiting".

I said, "My complaint is that what you've just listened to on that machine your shop sold me, is not the voice of myself doing it back to you. Not only is it not the voice of myself, whoever it is that is doing it, is not even saying what I said. So it appears to be faulty on a number of fronts.

Then she tried to be clever, "Where did you get the cassette tape from?"

[105]

I said "I got it from Harry Underwoods". Who she'd never heard of. I said "You know Harry Underwoods. The second hand shop on Whitfield Street. Next door to where the school used to be they knocked down."

She said, "I don't remember a school on Whitfield Street".

I said, "They've knocked it down, I've just told you.

She said, "This cassette is a very old cassette. It's obviously a recording of someone else that was on the tape when you bought it.

I said, "Well thank you! I knew it couldn't be me. I'm not a woman for a start, despite your inferences to the contrary about black patent stiletto shoes".

She said, "What do you want to do about it?"

I said, "I'll have my money back please. I have absolutely no confidence in the technology as advertised".

I've never know anything like it. And I dictated a lovely bit this morning and that's gone forever

Write letter to
M P about wom
in Angos.

now. By rights I should be constipated by Argus for that. I'm all behind now.

Anyway fair doo's to them, they gave me my £12 back. Si So I've had to come back to thumping this thing. That'll be tomorrow though. I've done my quotient for today. Well just about. Just coming up to about what you said I had to do every day without fail. Which I'm almost there with now. Just another seven words by my reckoning reckoning reckoning reckoning, reckoning! There we are! That's me finished.

And despite all that with the cassette player, I still managed to write all my words for today. Plus this extra bonus paragraph explaining that. Wonderful.

Should be due more money for that

CHAPTER 21

MOTIVATION

PEOPLE OFTEN SAY TO ME bugger forgot to turn
the capitals off AGAIN. Why have they put that
there? Where it's easy to forget? There's such a
bad layout on typewriters. They want a complete
redesign.

People often say to me, 'Arthur, you have had
such a long and varied career how is it you
keep yourself motivated up?' And that's a very
interesting question and incidentally the title
of this chapter. A device I have been using
throughout this book, for all you budding
writers out there.

Well that's a very interesting question.
(The one about me motivating myself up) And
coincidentally in my spare time, as well as
my lay preaching, I am a motivational guru,
available for block bookings and one to one
consultations. Things like getting football
teams to win games. Although getting Leeds United

out of the bloody Championship is probably a
step too far even for someone with my prowessess.
But seriously though, If they want to get in
touch with me now Neil Warlock has got the push,
I'm sure I can make them win the World Cup next
time Leeds are in one.

Now, I do motivational talks all over the place,
Tooting, etcetera, everywhere. In fact I'm lauded
and revered for it. And I always start my talks
off with this little speech to insipid people. `inspire`

"Hello everybody. Count Arthur Strong
Motivational gugu here. Before I start I'd just
like to say that, if during my introduction
speech you feel moved to tears. It's good to cry.
Let it all flow out of you. As long as it doesn't
go on. That's indulgent and annoying and there
is a fine line to not be stood over, with regards
to that.

You know, when I was a little lad, I used to sit
and read about the top film stars and matinee
idols of the day, and I used to think to myself,
It could never happen to me. And then I used to
think, well why not? And then I used to think,
because things like that just don't happen to me.

And then I used to think, but that doesn't mean
that they can't. And then I used to think, oh I'm
just being stupid and then I used to think, now
who are you calling stupid and then I used to
think, 'Come over here and say that!'. And I would
have gone on forever, if the bus hadn't come. What
I'm trying to say everybody, is that the power to
change course lies firmly, very firmly within you.

Now I know it'll be hard for some of you to
imagine, because of who I am and what I've gone
on to become, but I used to suffer from low self
esteem about myself. And if I found myself in a
room full of empty people, I wouldn't know what
to say and pretty soon that room full of people
would be an empty room full. What you have to
do is focus and be positive. You see when I look
at a half empty glass, it doesn't look half empty
to me. It looks half full. Well the bottom half
of it does. Obviously the top half of the glass
is half empty, but that's not not the half I'll be
drinking. That would be stupid. It would just be
air. And you can't drink air can you? Mind you
it would be marvellous if you could wouldn't it?
Although that would make air, water wouldn't it?
So that would be like being underwater, and we

get chewing gum

don't have gills like a cod does, so you'd possibly die? Well you might die but I'm a half a glass half full man so I wouldn't, because I think I've got liquid in a glass? Haven't I? Also if air were drink all the pubs would close down. So there are all those implications to weigh up as well. Really it's probably not worth it.

Now if you like what you've just read, why don't you book up for the chance to turn your life around and make something of yourself for once?

Instead of always being in a room full of people by yourself, tongue tied and wanting to go to the lavatory when any body speaks to you, you could be just like me. Well you might still need the toilet but you won't be tongue tied. Of that I can assure you."

I'll put one of my flyers in between the pages, if they let me, and all the information you need is on there. Not that I'm touting for work.

Here follows some testimonials from top celebrities who have benefitted from me. They are completely unsolicited and a big surprise to us all when they came in the post.

MELVIN HAYES

I just want to say that when I was in 'Summer
Holiday' with Cliff Richards I was motivated
up by Count Arthur and even though I am quite
small they let me drive the bus once, although
it was cut from the film. I've never looked back
since and look forward to another job with eager
anticipation.

CHRIS AKABUSI

My hurdling was literally all over the shop
until I had a one to one with Count Arthur
Strong. I then went on to win the bronze, I think,
at the Olympics or Commonwealth Games. Bless
you Count Arthur. Whatever you charge it's not
enough. You could easily double it.

UNA STUBBS

'I was in 'Summer Holiday' with Melvin Hayes, (see
above) and what he says is true. About the bus.
Coincidentally, I also saw the Olympics when
Chris Eubank won the bronze hurdles, and that's
true as well. Count Arthur helped me overcome
stage fright and I can honestly say, with my
hand on my heart, that I'm not bothered by stages
at all now or anything'.

Oh dear they're really embarrassing me those letters and I do wish they hadn't put them in. I'm just a simple man with a gift who might be able to help you for a small fee of money.

Anyway, it's up to you. As I say I'm not touting for work and I do one to one's and block bookings. All the numbers are on the flyer.

CHAPTER 22

THE CUCKOO IN THE NEST

I just overheard a woman I don't talk to in Iceland saying that Carol Vordeman had broken her nose. So you heard it here first.

In an associated matter, I've written up to Countdown about getting on it, but they haven't even bothered replying. I'm good at the conundrums. Plus I'd be electric in 'Dictionary Corner' or hosting it. I don't know how him off The Apprentice got on it? What does he know about Countdown? I hardly watch it now. I bet a lot of people have stopped watching it. What's his name? Him off the Apprentice?

They want to take a leaf out of Marks and Spencers book, whose response to a letter of mine I now reproduce for you verbatim.

Dear Mr Marks or Spencer,

I hope you two can live with both of yourself's.

This morning I purchased a pack of your assorted
nuts you do for one pound twenty a throw. So
far so good. Alas though, unbeknownst to me, my
horror story was only just about to begin.

On opening the container, I observed, with some
satisfaction, a Brazil nut, a personal favourite
of mine, on the top of the pile, which I ate
with some relish. I clearly remember thinking,
"I shall enjoy another one of those shortly, as
I work my way through the so-called assortment,
watching Bargain Hunt".

It was just after we found out who the experts
are today, (FYI, Phillip Serrell, who I'm not
that keen on and Anita something from Scotland,
ditto), that I realised the full implications
of what was going on. I regret to inform you
that, that, that Brazil Nut was the only one of
it's kind amongst the so-called assortment. Now
it clearly states on your labelling, and I'm
reading off the pot now, as we speak:

Nut Assortment. Ingredients.

Almonds (25%) - Brazil Nuts 25% - Cashew Nuts (25%) - Hazelnuts (25%).

In my estimation I would say that it was more like:

Almonds (40%) - Cashew Nuts (35%) - Hazelnuts - (24%) - Brazil Nuts (1%).

I'm sure you can see the unfairness of all this and am interested to know what you intend to do about my debacle. The ball is now in your tennis court.

Yours in earnest,

Count Arthur Strong

MARKS &
SPENCER

Retail Customer Services
Chester Business Park
Wrexham Road
Chester
CH4 9GA

Tel: 0845 302 1234
Fax: 0845 303 0170
www.marksandspencer.com

Count Arthur Strong
1 North Parade
FROME
Somerset
BA11 1AT

Our Ref: 1-434269780
26 March 2013

Dear Count Strong

Thank you for taking the time to contact us. I am sorry to hear you were disappointed with
the quality of the assorted nuts you bought from us recently.

Quality is extremely important to us. We have strict quality control arrangements with all our
food suppliers to ensure every portion reaches the same high standards and includes the
right amount of each ingredient. However, there has clearly been a problem here.

I have passed the details on to our Buying team. They will follow it up with our supplier and
do everything they can to make sure it doesn't happen again.

I would like you to have the enclosed gift card for £5 as a full refund. This comes with my
sincere apologies and best wishes.

Thank you very much for bringing this to our attention. If you have any other queries, please
don't hesitate to contact us.

Yours sincerely

Jessica Albiston
Customer Adviser
Retail Customer Services

Marks and Spencer plc
Registered Office:
Waterside House
35 North Wharf Road
London W2 1NW
Registered No. 214436
(England and Wales)

PRODUCED ON 100% RECYCLED PAPER
MS&00059

Dear Marks and Spencer's,

Re Count Arthur Strong's lack of Brazil nut's comlpaint.

Many thanks for for the gift card you sent for the sum of five pounds which will come in most useful and I intend to put towards possibly some underpants next time I come into town. Or socks.

FYI. You might want to think about keeping your eye on the amount of chicken in your 'Chicken, Mushroom and Rice Soup', which can prove to somewhat erratic at times. Having left me both, ecstatic and disappointed in equal measure in the recent past.

This is not an official complaint, and I'm not after another gift card at this point. I am merely mentioning it to be helpful as I feel we now have that kind of relationship. If you did think it was worth a fiver that would be entirely up to thee.

Your obedient servant

Count Arthur Strong

CHAPTER 40

QUEEN OR KING AND COUNTRY

I'll never for get the date when my National
Service conscription papers fell like a
turbulent waterfall through the sluice gate
that was our letterbox. It is etched permanently
on my mind. I opened the envelope with trembling
hands. It said I was to report to somewhere for a
medical check up the following morning.

At 6 o'clock that following morning I left the
house, got on my bicycle and cycled to the town
hall somewhere, where the medical was to take
place. In a kind of daze, I stood in line, dropped
my trousers, (I'll gloss over what they asked me
to do then). And was passed A1 fit for battle,
despite having a bad limp (My Dad's idea).

I was given three days and told to report to
Catterick Army barracks, which was to be my home
for the next six weeks, whilst I was being honed
into a fighting machine. After that I was told
I would be posted. Which surprised me because I

didn't know you could post people. I'd imagined that the Army had a better way of doing it. It must cost quite a bit if you think of it.

Mind you, in those days postage was a lot cheaper than it is now. Goodness knows how much it would cost to send an actual person these days. It costs an arm and a leg to send a letter, let alone to send two arms and two legs. Plus all the other bits, feet, knees, head, etc. Hair isn't heavy.

Anyway, whatever it costs to send an arm and a leg it doesn't matter because I'd misunderstood what the sergeant major said and it was a different kind of 'posting' he was talking about. He made that abundantly clear to me when I said I couldn't be wrapped up because of claustrophobia.

Three days. Three short days before I was plucked away from everything I knew. Like a leaf is wafted off a dandelion by the warm summer breeze. So I too was going to be wafted into the army. In many ways I knew so much, but in other ways I knew so little. For instance I could mind read and had a phenomenal memory. For the last year I'd been gaining quite a reputation on

the Variety circuit as 'Count Arthur Strong the
Memory Man'. On the other hand I was a sensitive
young man, not unlike John Mills when he played
the grown up Pip in a Christmas Carol.

The three little days passed so, so, so quickly
and before I knew it I was reporting to Catterick,
a brown paper parcel containing my few precious
belongings tucked under my nervous arm.

I was told to go to the quartermasters, by the
shouty sergeant major, to be kitted out with my
uniform. It was there, in the queue that I bumped
into someone who would become a lifelong friend.

Brian Connely, not the comedian off the telly or
the blonde one out of Sweet, and, actually I'm a
bit fed up of hearing about those two whenever
I mention Brian. This Brian Connely I'm talking
about, was the same age as me though not as
privileged. He came from a rough working class
family, whilst I, it was rumoured, was a direct
descendant of a one time Lord Mayor of somewhere
in the Forest of Dean, who owned a chain of
shoe shops. But for all my good fortune with my
rumoured lineage, Brian had one thing I did not.
A trumpet.

[121]

We got kitted out and by the time we got back to the barracks we were chatting like old friends. A couple of the other fellas, Keith Moon (not the one out of The Who) and Stuart Granger (not the one off the films with the grey sideboards) could play the washboard and stand up bass, respectively, and I thought I might be able to play the piano. I mean how difficult could it be? We had an upright piano at home and I walked past it often enough. It seemed to me it was only a matter of stopping in front of one and putting the lid up. So we decided to form a tea band, like Spike Milligan did in his book, only better.

Unfortunately the training was relentless. And they used to make us get up at the crack of dawn. Getting up at six in the morning was an anamathema to me. I was used to staying up late performing two or three shows a night and then having a lie in until dinner time. Something I tried to explain to the shouty man. But he made me peel a big sack of potatoes. Which I thought was a bit odd.

They did make you do some strange things in the army. You had to shine your shoes with the back of a hot spoon. If you were naughty they made you peel potatoes or paint coal white. Which I couldn't see the logic of. I mean if you're going to paint coal, it should be a nice Sea Blue or something. Coral Delight. Something from that side of the colour wheel.

I still have nightmare's about peeling potatoes. The Doctor say's it's like a form of shell shock except with a potato. A kind of potato shock. They try to brush all that under the carpet but I bet there's a lot of ex army lads suffering in silence. You never hear anything about that on poppy day do you? And I've written to the British Legion about it. Nothing! I wrote, 'If Marks's and Sparks's can give me a five pound gift card for a Brazil nut shortfall surely the Legion can work some constempation out compenstation'.

I still have repetitive arm syndrome from holding the peeler as well. But you'll not hear me complaining. I was only too happy to serve King and country. Or Queen and country, whichever of them was on the throne whenever this was.

'On the throne' can also mean 'On the toilet'

Anyway our six week training raced by in a blur of whitewashed potatoes and peeling coal, and before we knew it, it it was the day of our postings, which I've already explained to you what that is. If you're skim reading and you've missed that, it's your lookout. It's nothing to do with the post office, I'll say that much. And frankly you shouldn't skim read anyway. It's insulting to us writers who put our life and souls into our craft for a good hour a day,. Every word part of an intricately structured journey. Leading us all, sometimes willingly, sometimes reluctantly, into the unknown.

Even now I can recall the trepidation with which I walked on my legs up to the notice board in the Naffi to see where they would be sending me.

'Strong, Arthur - Alexandria'

it said on the list.

"Look at that, they've got my name wrong" I said. "And anyway Alexandria's a woman's name."

"No," said Brian said, "Alexandria is a place."

"Where is it?" I implored him. To tell me. "It's not in bloody Scotland is it?"

I remembered what the audiences had been like up there and was in no hurry to return, to have more things thrown at me. If that was possible. I didn't mind the edible things, but because it was Scotland, most of it was past it's sell by. I once had the skin taken off my ear by a satsuma that must have been at least a year old I would estimate. That was the Kings, Glasgow.

Not like Buxton Opera House. The fruit was beautifully fresh there. Everyone wanted to play Buxton Opera House. In fact most of the acts took a carrier bag onstage with them. It was there I remember, I first tasted a lychee.

"No Arthur, it's not in Scotland, Charlie replied, "Alexandria is on the other side of the world, in Egypt, near Australia and look I'm going there too!

I looked, it was true. They couldn't have called us both women's names by mistake. We were going to Egypt near Australia!

CHAPTER 40

THE LAND OF THE PHARAOES

I'll never forget walking down the steps of that
old Dakota aeroplane. It was like walking down
any other set of steps I'd walked down before but
with one difference. Egypt was at the bottom this
time, not the downstairs cellar.

Oh Egypt! Little did I know just how large a part
this wondrous place was to play in my life and
I'll do that bit in a minute. But first there were
my duties to do, to do.

We were told to assemble for a briefing at 15.00
hours o'clock, which we duly did.

It's often been said about me that I lead a
charmed life, and I think there's some truth
in that. Never had that been more evident than
during this next bit I'm about to tell you about.

Our Commanding Officer was an affable chap who
I'll call, Captain Something, because his name
just escapes me for the minute, and as he walked

Captain Somethin

along the line and inspected us he stopped in
front of me for what seemed like an age, all the
time eying me in my eye. After what seemed like
another age he said, "Don't I know you?".

" I don't think so sir" I replied smartly saluting,
in the British fashion. Longest way up, shortest
way down.

"I used to be theatre manager at the Watford
Palace (I think it was)", he said (not the bit
in brackets) (he didn't say that) (the bits in
brackets are for clarity). (Don't actually print
anything that's in brackets in this bit). (From,
'I think it was', to the end of this word). (and
if you'd supply me with some more tippex I'd
have been able to tippex that out, instead of
having to go to these ridiculous lengths to make
it clear. All this has snowballed out of all
proportion now because of you). (And don't include
that neither). (or that) (or this).

Oh anyway, to cut a long story short. He
remembered me doing my act and asked me to put
some shows together to entertain the troops,
like in Spike Milligan's book again. Not that
I'm copying that. In fact I can hardly remember

Stamps

[127]

reading it. So you can forget any legal actions if you're Spike Milligan or his publisher and you're reading this. As you'll have probably gathered by now, this is a much more high brow enterprise than your book. No offence intended. The only similarity is, and I hold my hands up to this, is that we're both using the alphabet. And there's not a court in the land would find in your favour on that basis. Almost all books use the alphabet and I'm amazed I'm having to explain that to you. How long have you been a publisher for. I mean that's just basic is that. Junior school stuff.

The weeks that passed in Egypt were some of the happiest moments of my young life. The Egyptians really took me to their hearts. You can say what you like about the Egyptians but the hossability they extended to me went before them, it really did.

Most of my time was taken up auditioning aspiring performers, writing sketches, composing music, I had never been busier or happier.

But I also managed to find time to get off and do some sightseeing. I'd always been interested

in Egyptian alchoholology ever since I'd went
to school for that bit, and in a break from
rehearsals me and some of the cast hired some
dirty camels and went to do a bit of exploring
across the inhospital dunes of the Gobi Desert.

Ah The Pyramids, The Sphinx, The Valley of Kings,
The Valley of Queens, and the tombs. The tombs! *falafels!*

Do you know if I live to be an hundred, I'll never
forget that night when we arrived at the cursed
old tomb of King Nephewcanezza, if I live to be
an hundred. At either side of the entrance, hewn
from solid granite, I would imagine, stood two
giant Collosassuses Colossusses Collossussess
Colosuses. (Hang on. I know. I'll come at this
another way).

At one side of the entrance stood one giant
Colossasus and at the other side of the entrance
stood another giant Colossasus. (see) (There's ways
round all that).

We stood in awed silence, transfixed by the sheer
scale of it all. Imagine that, the entire cast of
Fiddler on the Roof struck dumb. It's a good job
it wasn't a matinee. I turned to Charlie, "You stay

with the dirty camels Charlie, (have I said we
had camels?) I'm going in the pyramid". With that I
made my farewells and flaming flambeau in hand
I turned and walked through the entrance. *who's*
Charl

Once inside I could half see in the half light
ahead of me a doorway. It seemed to beckon me.
Onward I went, ever onward, passing several
of the Royal sarschopagooses sarsophageeses
Sarsosagies? (It must be sarsophageese if there's
more than one of them? One goose is a goose, two
geeses is a geese. It's a plural) Sarsophageese.
Above them were writ the hieroglyphics 'Abandon   *Writ*
hope all ye who enter here' Beware the curse of   *to*
the Mummy's tomb!' I'd come too far to turn back   *Counte*
now. Onward I went, ever onward until finally I
arrived at the entrance of the burial chamber of
King Nephewfanezza.

Once inside there were no prizes for guessing
which was Nephewcanezza's Sarsophagoose
(singular). It shone like solid gold in the half
light, almost half blinding anyone who even half
looked at it. To my left, hidden to the naked eye,
I spotted a concealed chamber. My throat went as
dry as a bone. Could this be the final resting
place of the most famoustest Pharaoh of them all?

[130]

Stampe.

Now I'm going to stop at this point, because here's a good tip for you for remembering all these stupid names. You turn the name into English and break it up into syllables. So, let's go back to where we were and I'll show you.

Could this be the final resting place of the most famous Pharaoh of them all,

'Toot ... the ... car ... horn' See? Tootthecarhorn. That's how you remember them! And there's a patent pending on that so I don't want to come across any of you going round saying you thought it up. Pacifically Paul Daniels I'm thinking of there.

I pushed open the door. What secrets would lie behind the

just like Bruce Forsyth trousers, only without making a fuss about it.

People often ask me where did the name Count Arthur Strong came from, and am I a real Count. Well I'm glad you asked me that because they explanation is very interesting and quite believable.

Originally the name was my Variety monica, from when I started doing my Memory Man act everybody knows me for. Then in 1960 something I was afforded the great honour of doing the Royal Command Performance and I believe, and this can be verified by Debrets and Wisden, I'm almost shure of that, I believe that by dint of the fact that the Queen mother called me 'Count' and shook my hand at the same time, that, that that made the title official.

Let's put it this way I've heard nothing to the contrary from the palace and surely they would have let me know if it wasn't?

Oh what a star studded line up there was on the Royal Command that night. Mike and Bernie Winters, Aker Bilk. He used to get very nervous

Trous
shoe
glove
2 pair
underpa
2 par
of so
ties
some
banan

did Aker, before he went on. I remember saying
to him in the wings. 'You'll never be a Pavarotti
Aker, but stick to what you're good at and you'll
eat 56 weeks of the year. Now have you ever
thought about wearing a bowler hat?" And do you
know he took my advice and he has eaten 56 weeks
of the year. In fact he's playing near me soon.
With Kenny Ball.

It was that evening I recall saying to a young
Cliff Richards, "Will you get down off that
staircase? If your mother were to come back here
it wouldn't be just you that'd get into trouble,
it'd be me as well. Now act you age, not your shirt
size!"

There was only one blot on that whole wonderful
evening and that was we had this American
singer, (that's what he called himself), Perry Como,
what sort of names that for a full grown man? *there should be an apostrophe here*
Anyway I went to his dressing room before the
show to see what song he was doing. He said, "Wal
I'm gon do, 'She Wears Red Feathers and a Hula
Hula Skirt'. I said, "No you're bloody well not".
I'd heard that on the wireless myself and I was
going to do that as the finale to my spot. I quite

liked the imagery behind it. He tried to crack on it was him on the wireless, but I wasn't having that. I'm not an idiot.

I'm not an idiot (bolder

Well things tuned a bit ugly then and we had a bit of a set to. It didn't bother me because I've done boxing. Oh he's a nasty man that Perry Como. Nasty, nasty, vicious man. Anyway he threw a right hook at me and I side stepped and I was going to counter with a left uppercut because that is the natural counter to a right hook.

Unfortunately when I sidestepped, I put my foot in the orchestra pit and I fell right in. Right down to the bottom. Oh it was very serious, very serious.

Thank goodness there was someone from The St Annes Jombulance Brigade there. They had to call an ambulance and everything and I was rushed straight off to hospital, where I received immediate treatment for a suspected leg. So you can see how serious that was.

Anyway I think I had the last laugh because the very next morning at least two Equerry's from the Royal Family came into the ward, where I was

Stamps!

recuperating, carrying a big basket, absolutely
full of fruit, from the Queen Mother herself, and
extending her well wishes to me for a speedy
recovery.

All the fruit of the rainbow

So I'm sure you'll all agree, I had the last laugh
there.

Apart from not getting to do my act, in front of
the Queen and millions at home.

At the Royal Command Performance.

CHAPTER (ABOUT 40?)

MORE EXPERTS FROM MY DAILY JOURNAL

Thursday morning, 19066
Start work at the BBBC. I'm doing a bit on a radio
play with Anna Massey and Anton Lesser. Who
seem to be in every bloody radio play the BBBC
have on. I tell you something, if I was a small
child I'd think that's what radio was. Those two,
banging on ad infinitum.

It's not like the BBBC was. We're lucky if we get
a cup of tea out of them these days. I tell you
something if I was Director General the first
thing I'd do on day one would be I'd be down the
canteen sorting the food out. Getting morale
back to what it should be after Watergate and
Johnathon Ross and Russell Grant, fancy having
an elephant in a room. No wonder they were given
the push. Anyway I'd sort the menu's out. Never
mind hob-nobbing with Alan Yentob. I'd be having
'Hobnob's with Yentob. Chocolate Yentobs.

And in a side issue, he's very small Alan Hobnob.

*Biscu
Liver
1 onio
punt
mil
Bount
Potatoe*

I walked past him in the corridor. If he hadn't said hello to someone I was with I wouldn't have known he was there.

I told them, I said, "I've had no breakfast this morning because I thought there'd be food on". There wasn't even a bottle of drink on. Obviously some people have never heard of the word hossability. You'd have thought that they'd at least have some bits of quiche. Something you can wrap up and take home with you when you've finished.

I once took a whole salmon home when I did 'Just a Minutes'. It must have been twenty pounds if it were and ounce. Salmon for my breakfast, salmon for my dinner, salmon for my tea. I was sick of the sight of the bloody thing in the end. Laid on it's plate staring at me with those cold accusing eyes. Playing it's bloody mind games with me. I went to Hell and back with that fish. I can still see it now, looking back at me from across the table. Tormenting me with it's barely suppressed insolence. In the end I had no option but to flush it down the toilet. Face first.

Of course Nicholas Parsons had the pick of the table, what with it being his show. He took all the cheese. I can still see the look of triumph on his face as he waltzed out of the door holding one of his great big balls in each of his hands, of Edam.

Mind you they were all at it on that show. Clement Fraud went home with at least 3Ibs of humous in his cupped hands. Poor old Pam Ayers only managed to come away with a half eaten Cornish pasty. She was livid. Swearing like a trouper. Me and Derek Nimmo had to pull her off the producer. That is a side of Pam Ayers I hope never to see again.

I tell you something when you're listening to your radios at home, you lot, it all sounds glittery and lovely doesn't it? Sitting there dunking your biscuits with your feet up. Or having a cream cracker with a nice bit of cheese on it. Once you get the other side of that metaphoric curtain, it's all for one and one for everyman all for himself each back there! Half the cast suffering from malnutrition. It's a wonder we can get the words out half the time.

I was saying to an absolutely ravenous Edward Woodwardwood, I think it's very short sighted of them not to lay food on. They'd get the best out of us then.

He said he'd only a two egg omelette with a few chips all day and he had to pay for that himself in the canteen. That's not my idea of a public service broadcaster. No wonder the BBBC's in trouble. I tell you something, if I was director general of it the first thing I'd do, on day one, is sort out the food. Lest we forget: 'An army marches on it's stomach'. And that was Winston Churchill or someone that said that.

Callan
The Enforcer
The Wicker Basket

Minder?

Stamp!!!

CHAPTER 29?

AFTER DINNER

RIGHT I'M GOING TO DO SOME CATCHING UP NOW I'M BACK
FROM THE KING'S HEAD, MY MEETINGoh sod it. How
many times is this bloody cap thing going to be
stuck on. I'll have to start all that again now.
It's a good job I looked up when I did.

Talking about food, as I was in the last chapter
before you say anything, one of the benefits of
being a celebrity like I am, is that we're often
asked to do After Dinner speaking engagements.
These can be for anything from a charity
engagement, like the World Wildfowl Life Fund,
or whatever it's called, a favourite charity of
mine, (the Wild Wolf something?), to a corporate
business do, for a lot of loud mouthed drunk
people who think they're wonderful. And one of
the first rules when you get one of these is,
you must 'Know Your Audience". It's meticulous
research that keeps these people coming back and
booking me again, hopefully.

For instance I did one for a chain of lavatory
bowl manufacturers once, no pun intended -
'Chain'. And I wish I'd have thought of that on the
night. It's funny how a lot of things occur to you
to say after the event, as it were. Even someone
as clever as me will often seem to come up with
a very acute riposte some day or so later after
the thing I'm riposting to has occurred. Often
coincidentally, when I'm seeing a man about a dog
in the smallest room in the house. Or toilet, as it
more commonly know.

For instance, when that bloody woman on the till
in WH Smith's says, "Would you like any of our
half price sweets or chocolates today?" The best
I've done in the shop was a curt, "No I don't! Stop
asking me!" Whereas if you give me a bit of time
on the toilet, I can come out with all manner of
clever replies, like, "Why is that you - Why is it
that when you, it you

I'll be able to think of one in half an hour. When
I do I'll come back to this bit and write it in. If
I remember.

Anyway, if I'd thought of saying 'Chain', I would
have been 'flushed' with success. A pun intended

[141]

this time - 'Flushed'. Which I did use on the night. To great effect.

This is what I'm talking about. All these references. It's gold dust when you're doing an after dinner. Frankly, I've done that many now, it's like falling off a bike to me. And you never forget how to fall off a bike do you? Or if you do you shouldn't be on the road in the first place. Or the pavements. That's just an accident waiting to happen is that. You see them on the pavements all the time now don't you. I had to stick my umbrella through someone's spokes on the pavement the other day. It's disgraceful.

Not falling off a bike! A log. 'Like falling off a log'. Why do people say that? That's even more stupid than falling off your bike. At least if you're on a bike, you're going somewhere. If you're on a log, I don't know what you're doing, frankly. I can't think of a single thing you'd be on a log for. So that's that maxim scotched.

Another thing about ADS's, as we call them in the business for short. It's short for After Dinner Speeches, if you're that dozy you need me to tell you. If you're not that dozy, then apologies to you. It's people like the thick one's that get us all a bad name. If you didn't understand that acronym then you're probably better off reading a comic or something. The Beano's a comic and perhaps you're more suited to that. I used to like the Hotspur and the Valiant. Denis the Menace is alright, though I don't like the dog. It's never *Captain Hurricane* made me laugh.

Another thing is you often get Royalty turning up at them. The Duke of Edinburgh is often there at the Fowl Wild World Life Fund thing. *that is quite close to what its called.*

I had a very interesting chat with him as it goes, because I had a bet with someone, who will remain nameless because it's not his bloody book is it? Last time I looked. It's not as though he doesn't have a shelf full of his own, which I can't see why anyone would want to read. They're just one half a story after another. But you won't hear me saying that because he is one of my oldest friends of mine.

Anyway one night on the way home from the public house, I had a bet with Barry Cryer about what meat was in a kebab. He said it was lamb and I said it was all sorts of assorted meats

compressed together, so it stuck on the stick.
Like a big kind of, lump of luncheon meat
lollypop. And we had a pint bottle of Mackeson on
it.

So a couple of months later I'm doing a ASD for
the World Wild Werewolf Foundry Fund, whatever
it is and the Duke of Edinburgh's there, because
he's the Duke of it, and I had an eureka Johnson
moment, because I thought, 'Wait a minute he's from
Greece isn't he? It's his national dish is a kebab'.
So I waited for an opportune moment, but one
didn't happen so I pushed my way in, and do you
know he was a lovely man and I asked him about
kebabs and he said I was right and what Barry
said was rubbish. And he said he would take me
out for a kebab because he knew the best place,
near Tufnell Park tube station. And that was the
Duke of Canterbury, I've mixed with them all.

CHAPTER 31

CHRISTMAS

Every year at Christmas I do the story of the
Nativity for the Scouts at St Aidans and one
year I got one of them to record it. I thought it
would be nice, as it's Christmas now, if while I
nipped out to take some shoes back to the charity
shop, my cleaner transcribed it off the tape and
I bunged it in here, underneath this. So that's
what's happening.

THE NATIVITY AS DONE BY COUNT ARTHUR STRONG TO
THE SCOUTS.

"Twas the night before Christmas and all the
children were in bed excitedly waiting for Santa
Claus to come down the drainpipe, when suddenly
in the east, a bright new star appeared in the
sky. Just then the Angel Gabriel appeared and
told them to follow it. This new star had not
gone unnoticed by the three wise mice, blind men,
kings! Three blind wise kings. They put gifts in
their saddlebags of gold, frankenstein, and a

big bag of sweets, pick and mix if you must know.
Meanwhile in Demestos King Herod was killing
all the babies, which was very, very naughty of
him and he shouldn't be doing that. So Mary and
Judas had to flee, but when they got to where
they flew to they wished they hadn't bothered
because all the hotels were full. And I know what
that's like first hand because that's happened
to me that. I had to phone Doris up and get her
to come for me. But of course in those days there
was no Doris. Anyway they managed to find a pig
stye and they bunked the night it that. Which I
couldn't do. I do have my standards. Meanwhile
Adam and Eve were dead I think by now, now I come
to think of it. So they'll have missed the wedding
then. But they might have left Jesus a bit in
their will.

I've actually just done my will and frankly it's
a bit of a weight off my mind. I was going to be
cremated, but my friend and butcher was telling
me, he was reading that they're making real
strides in cloning, and one day they might be
able to re-animate people from just a bit of them.
So I'm thinking I might be buried now. I was going
to have, 'Not Dead Only Sleeping' on my grave

[146]

stone, but I might have to probably have to have something like, "Can you be a bit careful round here because they might re-animate me'. 'Your cooperation is greatly appreciated'. Or if that costs too much, because some of these Monumental Masons charge by the letter, I suppose I could keep most of the first one and have, 'Not Dead, just awaiting re-animation'.

Then Santa Claus turned up and got all the presents out and there was much mirth and merriment. Now get yourselves off home. Where's the vicar with that communion wine?"

CHAPTER 41

PANTOMINE

One of the things that I love about performing is the interaction with an audience. And there's nothing better for that than pantomine. Over the years a pantomine role I've made my own is that of Robin Hood in Babes in the Woods.

Now everybody knows about Robin Hood. He stalked the streets of Whitechapel in the dead of night, looking for his next victi

CHAPTER 41

PANTOMINE

One of the things that I love about performing is
the interaction with an audience. It really can't
be beaten. And there's nothing better for that
than pantonime. Over the years a pantomine role
I've made my own, is that of Robin Hood in Babes
in the Woods.

Now everybody knows about Robin Hood. He lived
in Sherwood Forest, robbed from the rich, gave to
the poor and singed the Sheriff of Nottingford's
beard in the Spanish Armada. Richard Greene
played him on the telly, which was ridiculous. I
would have been a much better choice. I had all
the costume as well. Lincoln green tights, tabard,
hat with an peacock feather in it, the lot.
Jockstrap. And I researched up on it all. Which is
I bet more than Graham Greene did.

    ROBIN HOOD FACTS.
    1) Didn't like women.
    2) He could have been a surgeon.

3) Michael Caine nearly caught him in that film.

4) He might have been Prince Albert.

5) Or he might have been that Victorian painter Walter Sick.

Wore a top hat

I was reading that someone had a theory that it could have been Hitler? Which is a thought. Someone ought to check the dates of the war and see if they match? There might be another book in that?

But whoever he was, we know he wore tights, knocked Little John off a tree trunk with a big branch, kissed Maid Marion on the back of a horse and slaughtered prossitutes in the backstreets of Whitehall. That much at least, is beyond conjecture. And it's research like this that comes in very handy for all those, 'Oh yes he is!' 'Oh no he isn't' 'Oh yes he is!' 'Oh shut up!' moments, that the kiddies just love to participate in when you're doing a show.

Had Walk si aut a sworn in i

I remember my forays into pantomine with great affection. One of my favourites to do was Cinderella. Which I was in at the Leeds Grand Theatre, possibly. Lonnie Donegan as Buttons and

Yana in the eponymous title role of Cinderellia herself. Danny La Rue (which is French for 'the road', if you're interested) was an ugly sister. And the funny thing about that is, that Danny was a man. (See photo of him with his thumb in my head on page(?).

Barry Cryer, who's a lot older than me wasn't in it, but I remember him getting a round in, in 'The Wrens' opposite, during the interval. Three pints of bitter, a small sherry, a barley wine and a Babycham for Danny. It's just stuck in my memory. I don't know why? Oh I do know why. He forgot my nuts! I had to make him go back. Well, you know, as I said to him, when you're getting a round in, you're getting a round in aren't you? Don't half do a job Barry. It's not the first time I've said that to him. Anyway, fair do's to him he went back and got them, and I wolfed them down hungrily.

We always nipped over road to the 'Wrens' for a few quick drinks during the interval. _milk_

Strictly speaking you weren't supposed to, but we were all top professionals so it was alright. And there was never any danger of us being late back more than on the odd occasion or two. Like when

Stamps !!

Yana, who never came with us because she was a bit snooty, had to cover for us for half an hour or so. Which she made a fuss about. As I said to her, 'You got to do your song twelve times didn't you? You couldn't buy that exposure. You should be thanking us Dana.'

We had two donkeys in that show that pulled the pumpkin. I would always volunteer to look after the livestock during a pantonime season. You could make a bit of money on the side bagging up their doings and selling it to people for their gardens. That's a little tip for all you budding actors out there.

I feel a bit like Peter Barkworth must have felt then, when he did his book about acting. Mind, I think my style of writing is just a little bit more accessible than his was. Although you won't hear me saying that. He did his best and that's all any of us can do. I mean when you think about it this book is full of tips. People will be buying this for it's tips. I might put that on the cover. 'Full of tips!'

Anyway, I was knocking the manure out for half a crown a bag, and there were a couple of rose growers in Leeds that swore by it. Apparently, they were telling me, horse muck, or donkey muck if you want to split hairs about it, has a high level of acidity in it, which is perfect for roses. One of the rose growers won a prize in a flower show in Wetherby, thanks to a shovel full of my two donkey's doings.

Despite the fact that the manure business paid better than the theatre, I just never got the same buzz when I was bagging it up as I got from being onstage in front of a live audience. So regretfully I sold the business (no pun intended) on. (Unless it's cleverer if I meant it?) I sold the business on, to one of the up and coming young dancers in the show, who was playing the part of a petrol pump, called Lionel Blair. The dancer was called Lionel Blair. Not the petrol pump. That would be stupid.

Lionel always looked like he could do with a good meal, so a bit of extra manure money coming in probably saved his life. Not that he ever mentions it when I bump into him. He got very grand since he started doing 'Give Us A Clue'. I always say be nice to people on the way up

because when you're on the way down you might
meet them again when they're on the way up.
And they'll remember that you never said thank
you for selling on what was a thriving compost
business with a large client base.

I tell you something it's a shame cat muck's not
good for flowers. There's about half a ton of
it in my garden. All round my mysanthracrumbs.
Everybody's got cats in my row. Them at the
end one's always having kittens. They brought
one round asking me if I wanted it. I said, "No
I bloody don't". I cut one out of cardboard and
nailed it to the fence because someone said it
would frighten them off. It's encouraging them
if anything. Him that sells the Big Issue was
telling me that if you get lion's droppings and
put that in your garden, the cats won't come near
it. Mind you, you might end up with a garden full
of lions and nobody in their right mind would
want that. So, swings and roundabouts really.

CHAPTER 42

STAGE FRIGHT!

Lawrence Olivier, Dustin Hoffman, Peter O'Toole,
Kevin Brannagh, Des O'Connor and Laurence Olivier.
Just some of the actors who I think I remember
hearing have, like me, suffered from stage fright.

Now usually someone like me would sweep what I'm
about to say under the carpet. But that's not my
style. That's someone like me's style.

I know people who have just walked off the stage
because of nerves, unable to continue with their
performance but it's nothing to be ashamed about.

I went through a period of having stage fright,
but I got through it. And here, in a bit of a scoop
for my book of mine, I'm going to write about it
for the first time.

It was in the early 60's. I was busier than I'd
ever been. It looked like with a few breaks I
would go on to become the household name I was
to go on to become.

[155]

I'd started not being able to sleep at night. I
would get into my pyjamas and go to bed but
just couldn't switch off. I would lay there, my
mind racing like a formula one racing car with
Jenson's Button at the wheel. Often I would have
to get up and have a second cup of Horlicks,
before finally the Sandman would conclude a
successful visit and I would slip into the land
of nod. But that's not where it ended.

When I did finally get to sleep, I also had a
recurring dream, more than once, that I was
standing in the wings of an old theatre in my
underpants with an empty whiskey tumbler in my
hand, about to make my entrance.

I still have this dream sometimes. I have no idea
what play I'm in or what part I'm playing. Or what
my lines are. I keep thinking maybe it'll all come
back to me once I start talking.

Brian Blessed is on stage shouting something
about car insurance. I look around to see Carol
Vorderman standing next to me. She asks me if
I want my debt's consolidating. The sweat is
pouring down my face. I can't move my feet. I look
to my left. A grotesquely made up version of

[156]

the woman from WH Smiths stands there. She has
lipstick smeared all over her mouth. Her yellow
teeth protrude, "Would you like any of our half
price sweets or chocolate" she intones. I begin *Brilliant*
to scream. I begin to scream. (That's not a mistake
doing that twice. It's for effect)

Fortunately, this time the librarian woke me
up and I hadn't broken anything in there so
she couldn't ask me to leave. And anyway it was
their fault. It was too hot in there. How you're
supposed to stay awake reading the Advertiser
when it's bordering on the sub tropical.

Mind you, from what they say it'll only get worse
with the ozone hole closing up. Which one's at *Ouzo*
the top? The Arctic or the Antarctic? Because if *hole*
whichever one of them's at the top melts it'll all
run down to the bottom one won't it?

Surely though if it did, it would all drip off?
If you get a football and a jug of water, and you
pour the water on the top of the ball, it would
just run down it, collect at the bottom and then
drip off. Probably into space, where it would most
likely evaporate. You don't need an 'O' level to
work that out. So what's all the fuss about? You

see there's an awful lot of nonsense talked about globular warming. I might write that up and send it to the Khoto agreement people.

That is the first time I've ever thought about it and I've just turned everything they thought they knew on it's head. And some so-called expert will be getting paid hundreds of pounds to sort the Ouzo hole out. Honestly you can't believe it can you? It's often been said about me that I'm good at problem solving. That's why I think I'd go down well on 'Countdown'. I might reapply and mention that.

Me. Backstage at Stockport Plaza carrying my coat.

A dressing room somewhere. Note hair dryer on wall. Not everybody gets one.

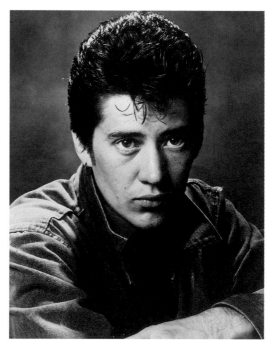

Elvis Presley.

PLEASE DON'T
FLUSH THE TOILET
DURING A
PERFORMANCE

PLEASE do not put the
blue paper towels down
the toilet

They will block it

Please put used paper
towels in the waste bin

Orders about a backstage toilet (above). The funny thing about it is, that 'going' to the toilet can sometimes be a bit of a performance!

NOTE LO59 DVA

A monkey on a car (a Nissan)

Me, Alister Kerr and Barry Cryer. As you can see he's quite a bit older than me. (Barry Cryer is)

Me with Danny La Rue. He's sticking his thumb right in the base of my skull. He's possibly jealous of me.

Katherine Hepburn?

Leslie someone.

Roy Orbison (The big 'O') and Dianna Rigg (The Mrs Peel)

Might be a Llama's behind?

Me and Roy Walker (off Catchphrase). That's not a stain
on my trousers. It's the lens.

Me again. Genuinely half smiling at something, half
funny. This is a favourite photograph of mine, possibly
taken by Lord Snowdon.

I have got more photographs. It's finding them.

There's one of me and Dora Bryan somewhere.

CHAPTER 43

DRINK AND DRUGS

The perils of drink have been well documented
over the years and show business has it's fair
share of big drinkers and hell raisers. People
like Richard Burton, Peter O'Toole, Richard
Harris, Marlbro Brandon and John Inman all
have a certain reputation, shall we say, for hell
raising. And it may surprise you to know that,
for a time I, myself, was a big drinker and hell
raiser. Fortunately though, one day I took a long
hard look in the mirror and didn't like what
I saw looking back at me (it was me) and said
'Enough is enough'. And so did the reflection.

I'LL NEVER FORGET again!!!! TIPPEXXXXXXXX! ← *Read this!!*

I'll never forget that time I looked in the mirror
and didn't recognise myself looking back at
myself. I was at my very lowest. It was sometime
in the mid 60's, I couldn't say when with my
usual precision, it's all a bit of a blur. I'd been
invited to what they used to call an 'all night

party' at someone or other's house. Or mansion probably. Most likely a mansion. (Possibly Vince Hill's but I couldn't swear to that). It was the time when I wasn't sleeping well. I'd just finished a show, I would imagine, and I'd heard there was a party going on, and the word on the grapevine was that it was going to be an 'all nighter'.

Stopping only to pick up a 'Party Seven', I jumped in a taxi and with the lights of London flashing by, like a kaleidoscopic strobe light, through the windows of it (the taxi), I sped to the party.

What we used to do in those days when we were going to a party was turn up with a 'Party Seven' and let everybody see you'd got it, so they all thought you'd brought some drink, then you'd hide it somewhere, drink everybody else's drink and take it home with you when you went. I've still got that 'Party Seven'. That's another good tip for all you actors to remember when you're at your premiers and TV Times awards do's etcetera.

Book awards as well now! I'll be going to all those with my Party Seven when this comes out.

[160]

Stamps

Anyway I got to the party and I'd been there
for a bit, a bit and I was just sitting cross
legged on the floor pretending to listen to some
'Hawkwind' or something, when someone sitting
next to me nudged me in the side of myself.
I turned round and someone that looked like
Englebert Humperdink handed me what looked
like, a really big fat cigarette about a foot
long. It looked like one you might get from a
joke shop. So I put it in my mouth and started
doing a joke with it. The man who looked like
Anklebert Dumperthing convulsed with laughter.
It was as though we were best friends, although
I always preferred Tom Jones. I didn't tell him
that though. He was my supplier and I had to
keep on the right side of him. Pretty soon there
was a crowd around me. They were all shrieking
with laughter. I'd never felt like this before. I
could do no wrong. I felt I was immortal. Little
did I know that what was happening to me was
what they call a 'trip'. The man who looked like
Anglepoise Humpaduck's big cigarette had been
stuffed full of drugs and I had become 'turned
on' by them.

'Bread' is money
in this language

bread
milk

Well, the next thing I knew, I was having an out of body experience. I was doing 'yogic flying', astral projection and everything. At one point I remember dancing wildly with Anita Harris, almost out of control! My arms flailing like a windmill in a typhoon. And all the time I was laughing. Laughing like a baboon. Apparently, I was told later, I tried to bite Rodney Bewes. It wouldn't have surprised me, so out of control was I becoming on drugs.

I'd never behaved like that before and while part of me liked it, wanted it, desired it, craved it even, I knew deep down inside that it couldn't go on. The only thing I could do was go for some cold turkey.

The next twenty four hours were the hardest thing I had ever done. Sitting up in bed with a plate of cold turkey, shivering under the eiderdown, imagining I was seeing things coming out of the walls. It was just like Ray Milland in 'The Lost Weekend' except I was doing it better.

switch the immers off

Finally though, finally, as the sun came up, I finished the plate of turkey. I'd got through it. I'd come out the other side. I was one of the lucky ones. Many didn't make it. It taught me a salutary lesson. Drunk and drigs don't mix. My advice is either do one or the other, but never both, you're asking for it.

Because of drugs, to this day I can't look at a turkey without feeling nauseas. Christmas has become all but meaningless for me now. Apart from presents and it being Jesus's birthday of course. If that's true. It's on the calendar anyway, so someone thinks it is and that's good enough for me. And I'd just got over all that and then some bright spark comes up with the idea of having turkey for Easter as well. Another thing I have to live with.

So in conclusion (to this bit. Not the book. I've still got about bloody 30,000 words to go for that apparently. Which is ludicrous!) In conclusion I had the strength to walk away from all that and I've never regretted it. It's why I've gone on to have such a wonderful career. Full of highs and some lows, but no illicit ones, except the one I have just been describing to you. But that was a one-off, that's the point of this bit. How many more times do they want telling?

CHAPTER 44

THE MUSICAL

My Fair Lady, Oliver, The KIng and I, The Sound of
Mucus, Cats, Dogs, Chess, Annie Get Your Gun, Miss
Saigon, The Wizard of Zo, Lis Miserabulous Lis
Miserableuos Mis Liserabuolous It's a stupid name
for a show that anyway. It's worse than sodding
Welsh.

Since the very first caveman howled at the moon
and blew on a flute literally hundreds of years
ago, man has always had the urge to set words to
mucus MUSIC. I'm always writing that instead. It's
because I've got a bit of catarrh at the moment.
TIPPEX! TIPPEX! TIPPEX! TIPPEX! TIPPEX! TOPPAX!
TOPIX! TOPICS! DO YOU GET THE MESSAGE?

Since the very first caveman howled at the moon
and blew on a flute literally hundreds of years
ago, man has always had the urge to set words to
music. It's what differenches us from the animals.
That and going to the toilet properly. Not going
where you're just stood up. And eating with a

[164]

knife and fork, that's another one I've just
thought of. Although I have seen a monkey doing
that. So perhaps not quite so black and white as
you might think at first glance.

Do you know, I think it was Sophocles who once
said to me, 'If the eye is the organ of sensation,
then the ear is what you listen to with, when you
hear something through it. Unless you're deaf
of course. then sadly, you're on your own. And in
this chapter everybody of this potentially award
winning book, I would like to celebrate that
wonderful theatrical genre that is the musical.

Music is a constant in all our lives. it
envelopes us wherever we may go. From the Royal
Albert Hall to the Asda. There's always music *All Bran*
playing somewhere.

They even have it on in the lavatory at the Asda.
Tom Jones was on the last time I was taken short
in there. 'The Boy From Nowhere' if you must know.
So you see, music truly can be a wonderful means
of communism.

Now ladies and gentlemen, it's my pleasure to
announce to you everybody, here in these pages,
that after many years of people going on at

me, I have finally succumbed and bowed to the incredible pressure and have finally agreed that when this book is finished I will be setting it to music and taking it to the West End (of London) as 'Through It All I've Alway's Laughed the Musical.' My musical director will be the Lincolnshire legend Ronnie Conway, who I alluded to earlier in the book when I mentioned my 'Doncaster' song, somewhere near the beginning. I don't know what page it was, before you ask. If you're that bothered you'll have to find it yourself. I'm not reading all this back. It's bad enough writing it. Anyway since I mentioned it before, Ronnie has phoned me up and unreservedly apologised to me. So, because I'm rather magnanimous by nature, I have decided to swallow the hatchet and revive the partnership that was so fruitful that summer season in Ingoldmells. So you can forget Rice and Webber. Strong and Conway are back in business.

But what really pushed me over the edge and decided me up once and for all to do it, was a very special letter I got, which I, at personal expense to myself, have had a facsimile photocopied of it which you can peruse.

1 Beckenham Palace,
Nr Pall Mall,
London,

My Dear Arthur,
        When me and my husband and I heard the
news that you will be setting your life story
to the music of Ronnie Conway, to be honest with
you, I felt like crying.
        As you know, you were good enough to send
me an autographed photograph of yourself, in a
good quality black felt tip, which has pride of
place on my sideboard. It really is a wonderful
converstation piece, and I just love explaining
to visiting dignitaries who it's of.
        You are truly a show business legend. And
I can't wait for this book to come out, when you
finish it. And frankly the news that one day you
will be singing it out loud on the West End Stage
(of London) delights me highly. In fact it's hard
to remember when I was more highly delighted.
        If you're not doing anything for your
dinner one Sunday in the near future, it would
be delightful to see you again. We can always
make room for you at our table. Edward can have
his on his legs. If needs must.

    All the best,

    Elisabeth R

    PS. Phil says to say 'kebabs!' Honestly, you two!

CHAPTER

THE 1970s - A WAKE UP CALL 46

Now I am a self confessed workaholic. Which is nothing to do with drink. It's to do with work. Work-aholic. It's like being an alcoholic without the alcohol and you work instead of drinking. Which on the face of it, now I've seen it written down looks stupid, but it is a good thing, I believe, the way I mean it. Though possible not quite so nice as having a drink? I'm split on that actually.

Never was I working longer or harder than through the 70's. I was one of the hardest working acts in the business. It was this guest appearance after that (guest appearance). Driving the length and breadth of the country to do a show. One theatre after another (theatre). I was burning both ends of a bitten off candle at once. It was more than I could chew. And it just couldn't last. Something had to give.

One morning, I recall, I woke up one morning with chest pains. At first I thought nothing of it. I often had chest pains and thought that this was another one of those. However this one didn't go away when I burped, like the other ones did, and by the middle of mid afternoon the pain had become like a tight knot in my tightly knotted chest. However I was guest speaker at a 'Water Rats' do that night for David Berglass, and I wasn't going to miss that I think it was David Berglass. He is an illusionist so it could have been someone else. Whoever he was, I thought, 'The show must go on', so I dosed myself up with an Aspro, or it might have been an Anadin I did use both. To be honest it's whatever came to hand when I was in the shops, it might even have been a 'Disprin', and on I went.

The next morning the pain in my front was back. I thought to myself, this is ridiculous and I reached for my St Anne's Jombulance handbook, off the shelf in the alcove to the right of the fireplace, as you face it, which I am Acting Captain of.' I then performed a thorough examination of myself with it. After no more than five minutes I reached my alarming diagnosis.

For a moment I just stood there, stunned, then I leapt into action, put my trousers on and telephoned my doctor, who agreed to squeeze me in. To see him.

Doctor Baker had been my doctor since I was a baby and he was something of a family friend. For some reason though, which I've never been able to fathom, he would insist on calling me Robert.

He said, "What can I do for you Robert?"

"It's Arthur", I said, "I've told you.

"Who am I thinking of then? he said.

"I don't know but it isn't me", I replied. 'Anyway, shut up and listen", I would have liked to have said.

"Doctor Baker", I continued, "Having woken up with chest pains two consecutive mornings on the trot, I was compelled to perform a thorough examination of myself from top to bottom using a medical dictionary I keep on the shelf in the alcove to the right of the fireplace, as you face it. Because of that I know what is wrong with me and I know what I need proscribing."

"Oh it sounds serious Robert", he said.

I said, "It's Arthur, and it is serious and if left untreated could prove fatal". I cleared my throat before I went on, "I have suffered, Dr Baker, from what I suspect to be an suspected heart murmur, and I've come in for a prescription for some of those, oh what are they? I've forgot what they're called now? Not Odour Eaters. It's a double barrelled name like Odour Eaters. BETA BLOCKERS that's it.

"I've come in for a prescription for some of those Beta Blockers all the snooker players are on. If as well as giving me a few extra years to live, it also helps to improve my snookering, then that's a side effect I'm only too happy to live with, my current highest break being somewhere around the 12 to 14 points area, in front of witnesses."

So anyway he gave me a prescription and later on I've gone in to Clarke's the Chemist to cash it in. But when I got to the counter it wasn't in my pocket. So I said to Clarkie, "Listen Doctor Baker has given me a prescription for some Odour Eaters. I must have left it on my nest of tables".

← Barmy
lawyer.
Celia
Imrie.
Biggins?

[171]

I said, "To stop me going back and fetching it, because in my condition any exertion could prove fatal, do us a favour, give me the Odour Eaters now and I'll drop the prescription off later on when I'm out getting my meat."

Well he's looked at me right funny has Clarkie and he's said, "You don't need a prescription for Odour Eaters, anyone can buy them."

I said, "Well what's Dr Baker playing at then? He's definitely given me one. I watched him write it out".

He said, "I don't know, but you don't need a prescription for Odour Eaters"

So anyway he's given me have a packet and when I've got home and opened them up, they're not for your heart at all, they're for your feet. I phone Dr Baker up, I said, "What do you think you're playing at, you lunatic? Giving me something for my feet when I've had a heart mumble". And I slammed the telephone down.

I said, "You want striking off you do. You're a danger to everyone". And I slammed the telephone down again. No use at all.

Stamps!

Mind you, credit where credit's due, they are
comfortable those Odour Eaters, I'll give that to
him. It's like you're walking on air. No wonder
all the snooker players are on them, the distance
they have to walk round the table. It must add up
to a few miles a match if you think about it.

Could put a photo of me on this bit?

*tin tomatoes
" mandarin
oranges
toilet paper
Stamps*

CHAPTER 47

STILL THE 1970s - AWARDS GALORE!

Whichever year this is I'm doing now, was a
wonderful year for me. It was the year I was
recognised for what it is I am and do, beyond my
wildest dreams.

Over the years, thanks in no small part to the
time I spent there as a child, Doncaster has
continued to draw me back to it. 1970 something
found me back there once again to host a cookery
programme on the now sadly no longer with us,
Doncaster Cable Vision. And I'll never forget
one episode of that show in particular when my
transmission was interrupted by a special guest
and I was presented with the inaugural, first
ever 'Donnie Award' for Best Cookery Programme on
Doncaster Cable Vision. This award, (A great big
wooden spoon with a bow on it, all engraved with
a lovely little face) still takes pride of place
on my mantlepiece, next to where the room for my
other awards is.

And do you know, I'd no idea I'd won it. They presented it live on air to me as I was chopping the ingredients for what has become my signature dish of mixed salad.

I was speechless, and it was very moving. Very moving indeed. I don't mind telling you, I had a bit of a lump in my throat. Piece of carrot it turned out to be, when someone had a look. We got it out, don't worry about that. The cameraman had to do the Heineken Manouverment on me.

Shot right across the room that bit of carrot. It's a good job nobody was in the line of fire, it would have taken their eye out. I was surprised it went that far actually. Very impressive. *Guinness Book of Records*

They got Matthew Corbett and Sooty to present my award to me. Well I'm saying Sooty, strictly speaking it was just Matthew. He had to keep his Sooty hand out the other side of the door in the corridor, because I'll not have animals in a kitchen of mine. It's largely a hygiene issue, you see. Because with a lot of animals, like mice, they do their mess as they're walking and it just lays where it falls, and you can't have too much of that going on in a kitchen. Health and safety would be down on you like a ton. A brick ton. *a ton of bricks*

[175]

After I'd got my breath back I was whisked off (that's an intentional cookery pun) to a star studded ceremony, where I made a wonderful speech, (my words not theirs).

Everyone who was anyone was there. Rounded of by the top pop group, The Wurzels. Who I'd never heard of until that night. They all wear clothes like they're dirty old farmers. In fact when I first saw them I said, "Who's let them in here? It's not a soup kitchen. You want to throw them out. Go on I'll back you up if there's any trouble" They were touching all the sandwiches as well. I shouted across, "Hey! We've got to eat those when you've finished fingering them. You shouldn't be in here you lot".

But anyway it turned out they they weren't tramps at all. They're a proper pop group. They've got electrical guitars and a speaker and everything. A broom stick handle with bottle tops nailed to it. They've got the lot. They bring it all with them in a van. That's all included in the price apparently.

Despite our little misunderstanding, I'm now happy to report that me and the Wurzels are the best of friends. Apart from the drummer who touched the sandwiches. He seems to enjoy bearing a grudge. I'm not that bothered. He's only about four foot tall. Little twit.

Anyway we'll have someone decent playing for the awards do after this book comes out. The Beatles? or Herman Hermits?

Hawkwind?

CHAPTER

SAMMY DAVIS JUNIOR - I SAY MY FAREWELLS

Because of all my awards and everything I was
now considered what they call an 'A' lister.
And what that means is that when people are
making lists, you, (me, not you), get to be near
the top of it because they use the alphabet
and 'A' is the top letter to be. It's like being
number 1 in numbers is. In fact it would be more
straightforward if they used numbers I think.
You know where you are with numbers. Obviously
one can't spell words with them, but that's not
what they're there for. Anyway I was at the top of
whatever system you like.

For instance, if I wanted to go to somewhere like
Stringfellows, like you read about people doing, I
wouldn't have to book a ticket. I could have just
walked in, like Rod Stewart or Vera Lynne.

What I'm saying is a lot of doors were open to me
because of who I was and still am. In fact right
up to today, I've never had to pay for meat in the

butchers near me. And that's because I was in an episode of Juliet Bravo and he recognised me.

Because of my fame, I was getting more and more public appearance work. Opening supermarkets and shoe shops and suchlike. I was becoming a terrible, busy celebrity. It was

Because of my fame, I was getting more and more public appearance work. Opening supermarkets and shoe shops and suchlike. I was becoming a terribly, busy celebrity. I've always been able to think on my feet so I was ideally suited to this kind of public appearance.

In fact I never wrote any speeches for any of these things, preferring the freshness of making it up as I went along. I comes naturally to me and always has. I once spoke completely off the cuff for two full minutes on where paper comes from. The teacher put the watch on me and everything. I won a lollipop. I can still remember it now, "Paper comes from wood, wood comes from the trees, the trees grow in the jungle, God made the universe Mrs Andrews?".

I think there was another bit that went in the middle but that's the gist of it. And I've always been able to do that.

It was whilst opening a shoe shop in Leeds, Carters Casual Footwear, that I got a telegram from mother telling me that her and my father had decided to emigrate to Austria. As soon as the doors of Carters was open to the general public and I'd done a photo session with Retail Footwear Monthly, of me with a brown brogue, I rushed back to London to say my farewells.

"Farewell mother. Farewell father". These were the farewells I said to Mother and Father. And they were the hardest farewells I'd ever had to say to anybody since we buried what was left of the goldfish, after the cat had it out of the tank.

I'd often wished that goldfish was a pirana and when the cat stuck it's head in it'd have taken it clean off. I'd never liked that cat since it scratched me when I was trying to put it in the fridge. And all this was flashing through my mind as we three stood standing there, not knowing what to say to each other. Finally one of us had to speak. To say what was on our minds.

[180]

"Won't it be cold in Austria?" I uttered my voice thick with emotion.

"Probably", my mother responded, her voice also thick with emotion, but not quite as thick as much as mine was. "What are you asking me that for?"

Leiderhosen

"Just that you want to make sure you've got some warm clothes with you".

"We're going to Australia! Not Austria"

"Oh" I said, thinking that I'd have to go back now and change that bit. And I might have mentioned Austria in the last chapter as well. I'm going to have to go back and look for that now. As if I haven't got enough to do. I wouldn't mind but I'm only getting paid tuppence for this in the first place.

"I'd thought you didn't get a boat to Austria", I laughed hysterically, only stopping to say the next bit.

"Well, I suppose this is it then?" I suddenly didn't know what to say, so I looked down at both my feet, which were where I'd left them. The new

brown brogues from Carters suddenly surprising
me. It almost looked like I was looking at
someone else's feet. But I wasn't. That wouldn't be
possible, that someone else's feet were there.

I'd forgotten all about the frenzied adulation
I received in Leeds, opening that shoe shop was
now just a distant memory in my mind. I looked at
Mother

Isn't this long enough now, this book? Most Enid
Blyton books are under 200 pages you know.

Oh sod it, I've forgotten to do Sammy Davis
Junior as well. I'm not doing it again

There's some room for a photo of me on the rest of this page

THE BATTLE OF BRITAIN

BY

COUNT ARTHUR STRONG

CHAPTER 1

Wing Commander Sir Herbert Mayhew, his rolled
gold cufflinks glinting as they caught the light
from the cut glass chandelier suspended over his
head which was covered in neatly trimmed thick
grey hair, reached into his solid walnut drinks
cabinet and selected a single malt whiskey.

He poured out two large ones out, and turned
to his colleague Sir Percival Lawrence the
Secretary of State from the War Office who was
leaning against the marbled mantlepiece smoking
an Kensitas cigarette.

"Do you take water with it Percy, I never can
remember", quizzed Sir Herbert.

"Just a little old boy, to unlock the flavour,
don't you know?"

[183]

"If I knew I wouldn't be asking would I" Sir
Herbert snapped.

Sir Percy raised his eyebrows. "I didn't mean
'Don't you know?' like with a question mark. I
meant, 'Doncha know!' It's what posh people say
to each other. It's what keeps us separate from
proletariat people that walk everywhere"

"Sorry old boy! I completely forgot we did that.
It's this war it's really getting on my nerves".

He handed the other one a drink and had a sip
of his drink whilst they both warmed their
backsides in front of the fire.

"Mmmmnnn. Not bad said one of them to the other
after sampling his drink. "Single Malt?"

"Glenfiddich. It's alright isn't it?"

"I usually prefer 'Oban' for a single malt" Sir
Herbert pondered.

"It's a bit 'peaty' for me 'Oban', ruminated
Sir Lawrence. "I'll tell you one I do like. I
don't know how you say it but it's spelt like
this 'Laphroaigh'. It's probably pronounced

'Laphroaigh'. Something like that. Mind, you'd
have to go a long way to beat a 'Glenmorangie'.

"It's a nice drop of splosh is a Glenmorangie.
I'll tell you though, if you're not bothered
about a single malt, what is a good bog standard
scotch blend"

"What is?" said Sir Percival.

"Famous Grouse", replied Sir Lionel. "And
the commercials are funny with that big bird
waddling about. What bird is that?"

"It must be a grouse mustn't it?" said Sir
Lionel".

"That would make sense", said the other one back
to the other one.

"Hey I'll tell you who's go an offer on bottles
of spirits"

"Who?"

"Asda's. Their own brand. Eight pounds".

"Oh I'll try some of that", he uttered.

"You need a voucher out of The Sun".

"I'm not buying The Sun".

"Well you won't get the offer then will you?"

"I don't care."

CHAPTER 2

Sir Hubert Mayhew pushed his shopping trolley
around Asda's looking for the drinks bit

CHAPTER

ROLE PLAYING

One of the things I do from time to time, to time,
to keep my hand in as it were, is I do some role
playing for doctors and vets and suchlike, when
they're training. I don't do it because I need the
money. I do it because I don't need the money.
And I'm giving something back to society. I'm a
bit like Zorro or the Scarlet Pimpernel in that
respect.

What it is is, I pretend to be a patient or the dog
owner or whatever, and they have to be nice to me.
Whatever I say to them they have to be nice back.
To prove that they can deal with normal people.

I remember I did one where they were training
vets, and I took a dog and said I wanted her to *a whippet*
put it down, because it messed on the rug in the *sausage*
hall. And I liked that rug, which I had to put in *dog*
a bin liner and give to the Oxfam shop because *cross!*
of that dog doing that.

She said, "Oh no, I can't put a dog down just because it's soiled on your hall rug"

I said, "Alright, it's chewed one of my shoes as well. Which ironically was a Hush Puppy. And I liked those shoes".

She said, "That's still not enough reason to end a dog's life"

I said, "What about this then? When I got home from work last night that dog had eaten a cushion off the settee and killed a gerbil which I was looking after for a small child who has croup. Now will you please humanely destroy it?"

She said, "I'm not putting this dog down for those reasons".

So I said, 'What if it cocked its leg on a pensioner?"

Well I could see she was having a good think about this because she had her head in her hands. So I threw in, "And it broke wind in church last Sunday".

She ran out the room shouting then. I couldn't repeat what she was saying but it was disgraceful.

Still as I said to the panel afterwards, that's another one I've winkled out for you.

Mind you, some of them are worse than her. I did one for some trainee doctors once and the first one said, "How can I help you?".

I decided I'd have an ear infection, so I said "I've got something wrong with my ear", I said.

"Oh", he said, "What's wrong with it?"

I said, "I don't know! What are you asking me for? You're the doctor".

He said, "No, I mean, what are the symptoms".

I said, "Well when I blow my nose my ears pop".

He said, "Mmmnn, could be sinus trouble".

I said, "I haven't finished yet. You're bolting my stable door before the horse has spoken". I said, "When I blow my nose my ears pop and because of this my hat sometimes falls off, and I get pins and needles in my leg. And I can't straighten this finger". And I showed him my finger which is crooked because I got it stuck in a deck chair when I was eleven. But he didn't know that did he?

some mushrooms are poisoness

He turned round to the panel and said, "This is ridiculous. These symptoms are just ridiculous".

I said, "They might be ridiculous to you, but it's a matter of life and death to someone like me". I said, "You could at least prescribe me a placebo or some penicillin or something couldn't you?" I said, "This is what's wrong with the National Health, this kind of attitude". I said, "I remember when hospitals were hospitals. And you had a matron, like Hattie Jaques was in Carry On Doctor. And she was in love with Kenneth Williams. He was scared stiff of her. She chased him round the hospital. He had to hide in a cupboard. I always thought they'd make a lovely couple. I think James Robertson Justice was in that one as well wasn't he? Was he? Was he in that? Or is it Doctor in the House I'm thinking of".

Well he turned round to the panel again and said, "My diagnosis would be lunacy".

I thought, what an idiot. How can not being able to straighten your finger and your hat blowing off be lunacy. I said, "Doctor Findlay would be turning in his grave listening to something like this."

[190]

See if we can get in touch with Dr Findlay for testermonial or the actor that

He just stared at me with his mouth open this so-called would-be doctor. I said, "Come on! You should know all these films about doctors back to front, you should. If you wan't to be one yourself. You've got to put the hours in. You can get them all on VD's these days".

I did used to enjoy doing those. Which I didn't do for the money. And I've had all the colours of the rainbow wrong with me for them. Scarlet fever, yellow jaundice, pink eye, red eye, gangrene, blackhead, purple bruise, blue tongue, black death. Oh that's twice I've had black. Turquoise eiderdown. No that wasn't one. I haven't had that. Where've I seen a turquoise eiderdown? Oh I know, it was on a washing line.

yellow fever? yellow river

Anyway, I'd be very surprised if any of the shower of doctors who examined me made it through. I know one of them's a security guard now. Simon. I see him down the Arndale. He would have made a terrible doctor. He's got no social skills. He doesn't even say hello to me and I'm the one that helped him find his true vocation in life. He should be thanking me, not ignoring me. I've done him a favour and probably saved a few lives to boot.

[191]

Actually, that's a point, I wonder if the company
I used to do them for have got the statistics
of how many human and animal lives I've saved
doing my role playings? It'd be a few hundred at
least, if not more. Thousands more like. But you
know I keep all that quiet and I don't do it for
the money, which is altruistic of me.

CHAPTER

STILL PROBABLY THE 1970s - ALL CREATURES BRIGHT
AND BEAUTIFUL.

Little did I know in the last chapter that those
role playings as a concerned poorly dog owner,
(for clarification, I don't mean the owner was
poorly. It was the dog) (it's obvious. If it was
the owner that was poorly it'd be the dog taking *Scratch*
me to the doctors, which frankly is the sort of *this bit*
stupid fantasy I'm not prepared to enter into).
I'll start this bit again.

Little did I know in the last chapter, that one
day, those role playings as a concerned poorly
dog owner, would stand me in good stead for a
wonderful job offer. And that was when I was
afforded the opportunity of playing opposite the
great Timothy Christopher and Robert Hardy in
that marvellous television series we'll all never
forget, All Creatures Bright and Small.

I had one of the happiest times doing that
show since I did my episode of The Archers.

[193]

Which incidentally is nothing to do with the
longbow as the title suggests. And, here's a very
interesting fact, Robert Hardy, who plays Sigmund
Freud in All Creatures Great and Beautiful, is
one of the leading experts on the Longbow in the
country.

Mind you there can't be much to be an expert
about can there, with a bow and arrow? It's only
a stick with a bit of string on each end and you
fire another stick from it. He's picked a clever
thing there to be an expert on hasn't he? There's
only three component parts. It's hardly nuclear
fission is it? He's getting away with murder
Oliver Hardy if you ask me.

You might as you say b; an expe on the whi and to

Anyway I told him something he didn't know. I said
to him, "What do you think of this", and I stuck
two fingers up at him, if you'll pardon my French.
Well he was furious because he thought I meant
he was to 'swear word' off, but I didn't meant that
at all. I said, "All right calm down. Keep your
hair on Sigmund. I'm just showing you something
that started at the Battle of Agincourt. Which
frankly you would know about if you were the
expert you crack on to be." I then went on thus:

This is true

Apparently during the battle of Agincourt, when our lot caught a French archer they'd cut his index finger and his middle finger off so he couldn't do his bow again, then they'd let him go. And then in battle the English bowmen would stick two fingers up at the French and wriggle them around to taunt them. And that's how we tell people to 'swear word' off out of it today. It's a French taunt.

Not that I'm advocating that foul finger gesticulations are the right sort of way of conducting oneself (by 'oneself', I mean you, to be clear). I merely report the facts.

And if you're a minor and you've picked this book up and read that bit, don't crack on that it's my fault when you get caught doing it. You shouldn't be going round sticking two fingers up to the French at your age. Behave yourselves. You're on a slippery slope you!

I had a wonderful dramatical scene in 'All Creatures Little and Large'. I was in a pub having a drink with my sheep dog, and Seigfried Farnham and Timothy Christopher walked in. Below this is a bit of the script, as near as I can remember it.

SIGMUND

Hello.

ME

Hello Mr Farman.

TIMOTHY CHRISTOPHER

Hello David.

ME

Hello Mr Herrieriot.

TIMOTHY CHRISTOPHER

Is everything alright David, you look worried?

ME

It's Bessie me dog Mr Herrierriot.

SIGMUND

Why whatever is it that's wrong, doncha know?

ME

Well I've give her the worming tablets and
everything, like young Mr Timothy said Mr
Sigmund, but she just sits around looking right
stupid and licking her privates. I don't mind
admitting I'm at my wits end.

TIMOTHY

Well tell you what David, why don't you bring her
in to the surgery first thing in the morning?

ME

Right I will. Thank you for that Mr Christopher.
That's put my mind at rest.

TIMOTHY

Good. that's settled then. Can I get you a drink?

ME

Lawks I don't mind if I do, young Mr sir. I'll have
a pint with you and no mistaking it. By the way I
like those adverts for 'The Sun' you do.

TIMOTHY

Thank you very much David. It keeps the wolf
from the door.

ME

I'm just thinking I haven't seen him in anything
for a few years. What was the last thing I
saw him in? Was it a 'Morse'. It was definitely
a 'whodunit'. Or was it 'Countdown'? Well it's a
whodunit in a way isn't it, Countdown? You have
to work the conundrum out. Someone like Morse

[197]

would be good on 'Countdown'. Or 'Rockford'. I
used to like that, 'The Rockford Files'. He had a
wonderful head of hair, James Garner. Who used to
get on my nerves on 'Countdown'? He used to wear
big stupid knitted jumpers with things on the
front. Whoever he was he was an idiot.

Doctors (!

TIMOTHY CHRISTOPHER
Here's that drink David.

ME
Who used to wear the jumpers on Countdown?

CHAPTER

TO HAVE LOVED AND LOST IS BETTER THAN NOT TO HAVE
LOVED AND LOST? IN THE FIRST PLACE? IT MUST BE
THE 1980s BY NOW SURELY.

With my elderly parents now living in Austria, it
was time for me to think about me for a change
and put myself first for a change.

For years I had selflessly looked after my
parents, but now they were no longer just round
the corner, or wherever it was they lived and it
was time for me to find somewhere else to take my
ironing and to take stock of myself. *find out where they used to live.*

I'd had no time for love. I was too busy with
my career. Work was my love and I it's obedient
servant. One day I was walking past a florists
shop on Tooting High Street.

I'd always had a green finger and I stopped
to look at some of the flowers in it. I looked
through the window and there I spotted the most
lovely woman I'd ever seen. The sunlight through

[199]

the glass just catching the wisps of the auburn hair on her head. She was just standing there sniffing. I often wondered who she was and that if I had gone in and spoken to her what would have happened. But I had a bus to catch. I had an audition for a Stork margarine commercial. What a fool I was. What a silly young fool. If only I could turn the back of the clock back.

There's not a day gone by since, when I haven't rued that decision. Perhaps we'd have been married now with children? A boy and a girl. Charles and Dianna. Or maybe I'd be infertile and we'd have to adopt. Or she could be artificially inseminated. I know there's not a high success rate. But we would have tried. We would have found a way. Me and whatever her name was. We could have shared so much, but it was not to be.

It was then and there I decided, like a catholic vicar, that love and marriage didn't go together like a horse and carriage for me, and I pledged that day to remain true to the one love of my life, as seen through the misted glass of a Tooting florists shop window.

On the plus side it's a Balti House now is that florists, and they do a very reasonably priced set meal for one. So you know, swings and roundabouts isn't it?

My Best fantasy cricket X1 ever!

Boycott
Vaughn – vice captain
Cowdrey
Titmus
Botham
Gower
Brierly – Captain
Trueman
Swann
Anderson
Root
Trot

[201]

CHAPTER

I LEARN A LESSON

It was in 1980-something that I learnt one of my
hardest lessons in life. Ever since I got started
in the profession I'd had the same top London
agent, Larry Trafalgar, of Larry Trafalgar
Associates. One day I realised that my 'Dixon of
Dock Green' repeat money hadn't come through for
some, not inconsiderable, period of time. Possibly
twenty years.

I'd telephoned phoned Larry several times about
it, but there was no answer. I tried to tell
myself that maybe he was on holiday and that
everything would be alright. But I new somewhere
inside, (of me), all was not what it seemed to be.

I decided there was nothing for it but to call
round to his offices and see what the deuce was
afoot. So I got the bus to Wood Green. The 147.

When I disembarked of the bus, I still had a bit
of a walk, which I didn't mind. It was a beautiful

sunny day and as I looked up a little fluffy
cloud sailed through the azure blue of the Wood
Green sky. As I turned into Larry's road a magpie
flew across my line of vision and I saluted it.
Not that I'm superstitious. I just think that some
bad luck might happen to me if I don't do it. I
should have saved myself the trouble.

Hello Mrs Magpie, how are you? And all the little magpies too.

Larry's offices were located at number 22. I
pressed his bell. A young man with a face on a
head I'd never seen before opened the door.

"Yes?", he said. "How can I help you?"

I said, "Larry Trafalgar please".

He said, "Sorry?"

"I said Larry Trafalgar. I usually go straight
through".

He said, "Larry Trafalgar? You mean the agent?".

"Congratulations", I uttered. "You know who you
work for".

He said, "I don't work for him. We're Steel
Stockholders but I know who you mean. We still
forward the odd letter to him".

[203]

Well I was stunned. "What do you mean, you still forward the odd letter to him?", I implored.

"Well we took over the office from him when he retired".

"What are you talking about, 'when he retired'? He's my agent! He won't have retired without letting me know. He's got all my 'Dogsick of Dick Greene' repeats money".

He said, "He's definitely retired. I know that for a fact. We took over the office from him."

"When", I enquired.

"Well, let's see. It must be about eight years ago".

"Eight years ago! Eight Years ago?" I though I'm not having this. "Larry Trafalgar we're talking about?"

"Yes that's right", he replied.

"Of Larry Trafalgar Associates?"

"That's the one".

"Small man with grey hair?"

"Yes I think he had grey hair".

[204]

Stamps!

"Glasses?"

"I think so".

"Wore a hearing aid?"

"Maybe".

"Walked with a limp?".

"He could have I suppose".

"Smoked a pipe?"

"Possibly".

"Terrible lisp?"

"He might have".

I said, "Listen I don't know what sort of game
you're playing, but that's not Larry Trafalgar
you're talking about! He looks nothing like that".
I said, 'Now come on. Spill the beans before I get
the police involved".

Well that shut him up. He's given me a right
funny look and said, "Look, this is our office. It
has been for the past eight years. I know your
friend has retired. Wait a minute". And he's gone
inside and left me on the doorstep.

After what seemed an interminable wait which
was broken only by the sound of Concorde flying
overhead, majestic in it's individuality, he came
back with an envelope in his hand.

"Here", he said. "This is his address".

I looked at the envelope. 'Leafy Glade Retirement
Home' Chingford.

I said, "Right well this better not be a wild
goose grease. If it is, I'll be back with the Chief
Constable, who's a personal friend of myself".

So, I had to get another two busses, because
I won't go on the underground until they do
something about the noise. They know that.
Finally I get to the sodding retirement home.

I go up to reception and, of course there's no one
there. I mean why would you ever expect to find
the receptionist actually at reception? So I ring
the bell, there's a bell on the counter, and this
person, who I can only describe as an idiot, comes
to the counter. And she looks at me and says,
"Shouldn't you be in your room?".

I said, "What?"

She said. "Shouldn't you be in your room? It's rest time".

I said, "I don't bloody live here. I'm visiting someone".

She said, "Oh sorry. It's been a long day".

"You're telling me it's been a long day", I confirmed. "Shouldn't you be in your room?' I'm in the prime of life I am. I've got years ahead of me".

"Yes well I'm sorry about that", she said. "Who was it you wanted to see?"

"Larry Trafalgar. Of Larry trafalgar Associates".

She said, "Right, well he's in the day room. Down there on the right. Or left. I can't remember which it was now. It's not important anyway. Let's say it was the left.

So I go down to the day room and I walk in and there he is. Sitting there reading the Daily Telegraph as bold as they come. I said, "Larry, what the bloody hell are you playing at? What's this about you retiring eight years ago?"

He said, "I retired eight years ago".

I said, "I know. I've just said that. Don't start saying what I've just said to you back to me. That will just look confusing in print".

He said, "Have you brought the dinners?"

I said, "No, I haven't brought the dinners! Do I look like the bloody dinner man? It's Arthur, Larry. Arthur. Why didn't you tell me you'd retired? No wonder I've not been up for anything recently."

He said, "Well it's very quiet. Even for Arthur Askey".

I said, "Are you on drugs or something? Of course it's quiet for Arthur Askey. He died thirty years ago. 16th November 1982. I was at the memorial."

He said, "What is dinner tonight? I'll not eat asparagus. I'll spit them out."

I said, "Look stop saying things like that. What's happened to my 'Dogsick of Dick Greene' repeats money?"

He said, "We used to have a dog called 'Lucky' and

my dad shaved it so it looked like a lion. Mrs Dean said she'd tell tell the police".

I said, "Oh right! I know what's going on here. You're trying to throw up a smokescreen aren't you? I've had enough of this. Larry, it's with very deep regret that I inform you that I am now considering other offers of representation. Good day to you. And with great dignity I walked out of the room.

So I get to the door and it's locked, and as I'm rattling it, some half wit nurse comes up to me and says, "What's going on here then?"

I said, "I'm trying to get out! What does it look like?"

She said, "Now you know the door's locked for the night don't you? Come on back to the day room. You can do a jigsaw before bed if you're good".

I said, "Listen, I'm not a bloody inmate. I've had all this on the way in. I've just been visiting him. That halfwit there".

She said, "Larry, is this a friend of yours?"

He said, "No. I don't know who he is. Have I had my dinner?"

I'd had enough by then. I said, 'Look I'm getting close to breaking point now I am. Of course you bloody know who I am. Arthur! Count Arthur Strong!"

And this nurse says, "Oh a 'Count' are we? I'm Princess Leia off Starwars. Pleased to meet you".

I said, "Where's her that was on when I came in? She'll vouch for me".

She said, "If you mean Julie she's had to go off. I'm covering her, from the agency".

So anyway, to cut a long story short I had to stay in overnight, until Julie came back.

Actually it wasn't that bad. I was pleasantly surprised really. The food was passable, I had Larry's asparagus as well, because he just spits it out, and I finished a jigsaw of Big Ben. Oh yes I've stopped there several times since. If you get there at change over time they haven't a clue. So you know, you could say I'm clawing my 'Dick Green of Dockleaf money back, in 'mini breaks' and asparagus.

And I decided because of how far back we go and
it's just the sort of person I am, to give Larry
one last chance. If he doesn't get me a part in
something like say, Juliet Bravo, then we shall
go our separate ways, by mutual consent with no
severance payment involved.

As an addendum to this, because I know you're sat
on tenterhooks about whether things worked out
with Larry, I'm delighted to say, yes they did.
And if you'll just turn the page, you'll find out
that he did get me an audition for Juliet Bravo
and I'll tell you all about it when you read the
next chapter, which is coming up as soon as you
like. It's up to you if you read it now, or have a
bit of a break, for say the toilet, a cup of tea, or
another associated activity. As I say the choice
is yours.

Cauliflower cheese
cheese, milk, flour.
make a sauce - boil a
cauliflower. Pour sauce
on it
Serve piping hot.

CHAPTER

JULIET BRAVO

I awoke from a deep sleep to hear the sound of rain pounding against the four paned victorian sash window of my bedroom window, when suddenly the telephone rang.

I looked at the Art Neauvo newvau neaveau neauveo wall clock, that I must have got from somewhere. It said 6.03am. Not literally, obviously. I didn't mean that. They didn't have clocks that could speak, in whenever this is. Well we had the talking clock of course but that's not the same as the kind of thing I'm trying to describe. That wasn't really a clock at all, the talking clock. It was a talking woman. I mean, she told you the time but she wasn't a clock, it was a woman. They should have called it, 'the speaking woman'. That would have made more sense. I'm talking about my Art Nuveau wall clock in my house. Which was a long time before you could get women that speak.

Anyway I put all this to one side and asked

myself, who would be telephoning me at this unearthly hour and why? It seemed to me that the only course of action available would be to answer the thing, so I lifted the receiver up and placed it adjacent to one of my ears, then using my voice I uttered. "Hello".

"Arthur it's Larry", the voice of Larry said to me.

"You know it's six o'clock in the morning don't you?". I informed him.

"Is it six o'clock?. Thank you. Goodbye". And he hung up.

I wonder what he wanted?

Another time he phoned me when he was on the right pills and it was a lot more straightforward.

"Arthur, I have an audition for you for the peak time popular BBBC television show, 'Juliet Bravo.' Be at the Hilton Hotel, Mayfair, if there is one, at 2 o'clock pm today".

Juliet Bravo. This was the golden chalice of television jobs. If you managed to get on Juliet Bravo you had it made.

I had to admit, that operating from his new premises at the old peoples home, Larry Trafalgar had really pulled it off. In fact I remember shouting in his ear trumpet to him, "Larry Trafalgar, you've really pulled it off". Which he denied. Saying it was loose when he picked it up.

The rest of the day passed in a blur. I don't mind admitting that even an old pro like me was a little nervous. There was so much at stake.

Apparently, Larry told me, I was up for the part of a policeman, so I decided, with my usual thoroughness and meticulousness, which I was known in the business for, to get a police outfit from a costumier acquaintance who owed me a favour, which I won't go into here, but it's partly because I used to clean her windows and she broke an Everly Brothers record of mine one bonfire night. ('Cathy's Clown', if you must know). So I went and saw her and I got a constables uniform. I actually wanted a sergeants one, because someone like me would have been at least a sergeant. If not a Chief Superintendent. But I don't know if a Chief Superintendent wears a uniform. Morse was an Inspector and he just wore an ordinary suit. Smart casual I suppose you'd call it. Well, whatever it was or is, I had to go dressed as a constable.

I was nearly late getting there as well, because I came across two separate cars, a red Ford Focus and a silver Mazda, both illegally parked. I had to give them a ticket. Well I would have done if I'd had any. I told the drivers to report to the nearest police station at their own recognisance.

Anyway because I'd done a bit of official policework on the way there I was well in character when I got to the audition. It was the best preparation I've ever done for a job and I would thoroughly recommend it to you aspiring actors out there.

I got to the place and I must have looked convincing because everybody kept calling me officer. Which I feel is a real testament to myself. And of course I played along with it because I'm a natural performer. I do wear a uniform well. Anyway, I finally got the assistant there to take me through to meet the Director, who wasn't right in the head if truth be know.

He said, "Is there a problem?" And I said, "Not yet there isn't", just as a joke, you know like an icebreaker. He turned to his assistant, who was a knife short of a full draw herself.

"What's going on?", he said.

She said, "I'm not sure but I think he's here for the audition".

I said, "Of course I'm here for the audition. Why do you think I'm dressed like this?".

He said, "I've got no idea, you're supposed to be a doctor".

I said, "What? A police doctor? Is there such a thing?".

He said, "I don't know. I don't think so".

I said, "Well what chance have I got if you don't know? You're supposed to be the director".

He said, "Look the part I wanted to see you for is the part of a doctor at the local hospital. It's nothing to do with the police force".

I said, "Listen, my agent definitely told me I was up for the part of a policeman. Why else would I be wearing this? I shall have to phone the old people's home up and get him to verify that."

Anyway the upshot of it was they were so
impressed by my degree of commitment I bring,
that they found a part for me in it. Of a porter.
I had to push a trolley past the bottom of a
corridor. Which sounds simple on the face of it,
but we had to do it about twenty or thirty times,
to get it just right. That's the projectionist in
me, for my sins.

So here I was at the very top of my game in an
episode of J B, as it's called in the business for
short. (It stands for Juliet Bravo). Not bad for
someone like me with such humble beginnings.

And also, on the way home from my triumphant
audition, I got a man to agree to voluntary
turn himself in at the nearest police station
for throwing a paper cup out of a car window
and I confiscated a recorder off a child in a
bus shelter who was causing a public nuisance
with it, and blowing it without the necessary
documentation. And when I got in, I learnt myself
to play Frere Jaques on it. Yet another string to
my violin string of mine I've got. Which, again, is
a metaphor before you say anything. I don't have
an actual violin. I have an imaginary one.

[217]

I don't have an imaginary violin.

CHAPTER 47

TOUGH AT THE TOP

After my succcesss in J B, (Juliet Bravo), I'm
afraid I rather let it go to my head and for a
time I burned the candle at both ends. There were
several lock-ins at The Shoulder of Mutton until
goodness know what time. Near midnight probably.
And I possibly didn't get up in the mornings
early also. I was living the high life, and I was
loving it. But it couldn't go on.

Fabulous though J B, (Juliet Bravo), had been, I
realised I couldn't live off its succcess forever.
I had to get back out there.

But, and you'll find this surprising

Good Afternoon
Good Afternoon
I use a nice pen.
A nice pen.

Gary Kane
and A
Tornado
Tornadoes
Tornad

[218]

CHAPTER 48

TOUGH AT THE TOP

After my successs in J B, (Juliet Bravo), I'm afraid
I rather let it go to my head and for a time I
burned the candle at both ends, a bit. There were
several lock-ins at The Shoulder of Mutton, until
goodness know what time. Near midnight probably.
And I possibly didn't get up in the mornings
early also. Thanks to J B (Juliet Bango) I was
living the high life, and I was loving it. But it
couldn't go on. When you burn both ends of the
same candle at the same time, eventually the fire
will meet in the middle and if it's your only
candle you've got then - well you don't need me to
tell you any more about that.

Fabulous though J B, (Juliet Tango), had been, I
realised I couldn't live off its succcess forever.
I had to get back out there. I had to get back on
the horse! ← *The horse in my head .*

It wasn't easy though. Strangely auditions began
to dry up. Word on the grapeyard was, that since

*Its not a real
horse .*

*I don't have a horse in my
head .*

J B (Juliet Bravo) My stock had risen so highly that everybody thought they couldn't afford me anymore. I had in effect out priced myself out of the market.

Larry did what he could but they'd only let him use the payphone twice a day in the home, for a maximum of fifteen minutes a time. Which I thought was rather harsh. As I tried to explain to them, sometimes he would nod off during a call, and in my opinion they should deduct any time he spent asleep on the telephone, off the fifteen minutes. But she was a right 'jobseworth' the woman I spoke to, and even though I had the backing of the European Court of Civil Rights, if they'd have wrote back to me, the old battleaxe wouldn't have it.

There was only one thing for it, either press on and hope something big came up, or go back to my roots and do a summer season.

It was a no brainer! I decided to get the old act out of moths balls and flex my variety muscles again, in summer season.

I still knew a few people in the variety

profession, so it was just a matter of making a
couple of hundred calls and, I was back. It was
an exciting new decade and I was back where I
started. In Variety.

It might be nice to
have a photo of me
here?

CHAPTER 49

BACK WHERE I STARTED IN VARIETY

Thanks to yet some more new drugs Larry was on, he was now staying awake for longer intervals, and using his old contact book he got in touch with an old contact. This old contact, who's name will come back to me, was delighted to offer myself a two week run on the end of the pier at Cromer, which is on the coast in, well I forget where it is exactly. If you look at a map of Britain - and here at this junction, I'll do a little pause to accommodate you getting one. And what other writer does that for you?

Plus I need the toilet, so that's worked out for both of us. Don't go to buy one though, if you haven't got one. I'm not going to do the full monty in there. It's just a brief modesty break I'm having.

Right, that's long enough. I was in there a bit longer than I originally intended. If you haven't got a map by now, it's your lookout.

So if you look at your map, it's in the bit that's
shaped like a head on it, on the right hand side.
I always think it looks like someone's sticking
their head out of the country, to peer at Belgium,
or Holland. Whichever's of them's opposite.

Anyway it's in the head bit, right on the coast.
Hereward the Wake lived there, if that helps.
And anyway, you shouldn't be asking me where
Cromer is in the first place. You should have
paid attention at geography if you want to know
where places like Cromer are. This is supposed to
be my memoirs, not a geography class. — *it's ludicrous*
I'm having
So without even waiting to find out where Cromer *to do*
was, I packed my suitcase, jumped on the train *all this*
and headed to wherever Cromer was. *for you.*

As the steam train? pulled in to Cromer Station,
belching it's smoke out of the thing that looks
like a chimney pot on top of the boiler bit of
it? I recall, I was a little apprehensive. How
would I be received by the other acts after my J
B (Juliet Bartrum) succsess. And it was with some
trepidation that I entered the theatre.

I needn't have worried. Everybody to a man, or

[223]

woman, pretended they were totally unaware of my televisual triumph and just treated me like I was any ordinary Joe off the street. Something I've always been grateful to them for. Though it wouldn't have hurt them just to say, 'Nice portering' or something would it. Or 'It was very moving when you pushed that trolley across the bottom of the corridor. It looks like a Spanish word 'corridor' doesn't it? Like Matador.

I slotted into rehearsals like I'd never been away and the next two weeks were some of the happiest times I'd ever had since the chapter I did about Juliet Bravo.

The other acts were, in no particular order, apart from it being the order I'm remembering them in - 'Des and Jade', a magic act, 'Derek Champagne and his Premier Crew', who did all the music, 'Sweet Georgia', two fat women that sang, The Krankies, and last but by no mean leasts, my good self.

I really warmed to the Krankies and got on so well with them. Jimmy the little boy one reminded me so much of myself at his age. And when we had a bit of time during rehearsals I would often take him to the zoo, and we would feed the lions and ducks and bats and whatever else you'd find in a zoo. Really, he became like the son I didn't want and never had.

I wasn't that keen on his mother though. She was a very pushy woman. I mean she was all over me, like she knew me. I only knew her to nod at. I actually felt quite sorry for Jimmy, they seemed to have no bond, him and her. She was never around when he was onstage. That's where we differed. My mother adored me, doted on me even, and it must have broken her heart when she decided to emigrate to either Australia or Austria.

In fact, I had an argument in a pub with some idiot about the Krankies recently. They were saying there was a woman in it. I said, "Don't talk rubbish. It's a little school boy and his dad, or big brother," I never did work that out. I said, "I used to take him to the pictures, little Jimmy". I took him to see 'Zulu'. And he could put some bloody ice cream away.

CHAPTER 51 ish

THE NEXT PHRASE

Before I start, I've just seen the headline on someone's paper that Abdul Qutada has said he would go back to Jordan? What happened to Peter Andre, the kick boxer? Dear me, she goes through them like a dose of salts, she does. She's been married more times than Elizabeth Taylor's husbands have had hot dinners.

And I was looking at the magazines by the tills in Marks's and now she's worried about her implants bursting, Jordan? It was on the front page. That's all you have to do these days. Have your bust done. I wish that's all I'd had to do, to get where I am.

I was saying to the woman on the till, why, instead of having an implant put in, don't they use a bit of inner tube instead? Then you could have a concealed valve somewhere, possibly in their belly button and you could pump them up to however big you wanted them, with a bicycle pump.

You'd need to carry a puncture kit around with
you for emergency's, granted, and possibly some
tyre levers, but they all have handbags don't
they? The 'super wags'.

file patent.

Imagine how convenient that would be. You know,
if you were going to church say, you'd let a bit
of air out, and if you were going to an awards do
you'd pump them right up. I'm surprised no one's
thought of that before? I might submit a paper
on that to 'The Lancet'. That's another thing I've
always thought of as funny. Lancet. You know,
like you lance a boil, and it's a medical journal.
Lancet. Lance it. They must have done that
deliberate?

And that's how I came to one of the biggest
shocks both in my life so far and this book. The
two go hand in hand. Haven't they got that by
now?

CHAPTER 52

BANKRUPTCY

In 1980 something I went to the bank to make a
withdrawal only to find that I had nothing to
withdraw. I was bankrupt. Bankrupt! In those
days there was a lot of shame, some might say a
stigma, attached to bankruptcy. I wouldn't say
stigma though, because I'm not sure what it means.
I have a good idea, but I'd have to look it up and
I'm too busy doing this at the moment. You go and
look it up if you're that bothered. I think it's
part of a flower?

And while we're on words, 'bankruptcy', is a word
which I actually think would look better without
the 't' in it.

Anyway I had no money left, however you want
to spell it. I'd never had to worry about money
before and here I was, having to worry about it.
This was a new sensation to me. I decided I had
to take a firm hold of myself and put my heads
together and come up with a plan to move forward.

I wracked my brains until finally I came to the unescapable conclusion that there was nothing for it but to auction off some of my belongings. Like they do in 'Cash in the Attic'. Except I wouldn't want Angela Rippon or Jennie Bond to do mine. Both news readers please note! Taking jobs away from proper celebrities. As for bloody Ben Fogle. What does he know about antiques? I have to turn the sound down when he's talking. On the plus side though, my lip reading is coming on in leaps and bounds.

I tell you who I do like though, Alastair Appleton. He's always very nice to the people on it. No matter how stupid they are. And he's on 'Start a New Life In the Country' as well. He's the same on that with them. Even if they haven't even put their own house on the market yet and it's obvious to everyone that they're time wasters, and think they have personalities and just want to be on television, again taking away work from people who should be on television, he just is very nice with them.

He started on 'House Doctor', you know. With Anne Maurice. She used to rub them up the wrong way,

"Your house smells as if a dead dog has weed on it. You'll never sell it if you don't get a new carpet and have the spaniel put down". And then he would come in and smooth it all over.

"So was that a bit of a shock then, when she said that about the dog". Compelling television and if Alastair had've been born in the past, whenever this is supposed to be, then I would have wanted him to do my attic now. Or then.

It is actually a bit confusing sometimes. Writing this now about what happened then, and trying to pretend you're writing it then. But you're writing it now. Still why should I worry about that. That's a job for my highly paid script editor they've made me have. More expense going out that could have come my way. Here eddditt ttthhis oout, iff yoour awakke!

Anyway I'm getting fed up of this chapter. So I wasn't bankrupt, I'd just put my wrong pin number in. I'd put 1490 and it's 1940.

CHAPTER 54

I, AUTHOR

I'm going to have to change my pin number now
I've put it in a book.

If there's one thing I've learnt in the process of
writing this autobiography of myself, it's that
you can't write a book in a fortnight. If you
take weekends off and Wednesday being market
day, that's down to eight days. And for a probing
piece of literary self exploration like this is,
that's probably a week too short. So I wish I'd
started a bit earlier now. I'll know for the next
volume.

A lot of you will be inspired to write your own
books when you've finished reading this, my
life's opus. Or volume one of my life's opus, so I
thought it might be useful if I logged down for
you the things things I have discovered during
the process of writing this wonderful, would be,
best seller.

Plus and this might as well be the first lesson, I'm using words up.

Now some people, like Barbara Cartland, Jeffrey Archer, Jilly Cooper, Barry Cryer, etc, get up at the dawn of dawn and crack on that they write 10,000 words before they've been to the toilet, which is rubbish and they're just saying that to make themselves look big. Are you seriously telling me that a person can lie in bed all night, for say 8 hours and then get up and not desperately need to ablute? I know for a fact that Barry doorbell

Can you believe that! I wouldn't mind but there is a sign up saying 'Don't press doorbell', and then they still go and press it. I told them. I said, "If that was the button for the nuclear bomb and you ignored the signage we'd be in all sorts of trouble. We wouldn't be having this conversation now for a kick off. And that would be your fault. Wilful flouting of a written instruction. Countersigned by me as well.

It's on batteries is that doorbell you know. Two U 2's. It's not for playing about with." He said, "Why have you got a sign saying 'Don't ring bell'

anyway? On a bell that works?" Stupid question.
Anyway I told them not to do it again. Delivery
or no delivery. I've lost my thread now because of
that. And I'm not reading it back, so I'm going to
start something else and that's the post offices
fault.

CHAPTER

SHAKESPEARE - THE BARD ON AVON

'If music be the food of love, give me excess of it,
that surfeiting my appetite will sicken and so
die. That Cassio loves her I do well believe it. Get
thee to a nunnery Ophelia. Nymph in thy orisons,
remember my dreams. Oh that this too, too solid
flesh would melt, thaw and resolve itself into a
dew. This septic aisle set in a silver salver, this
teeming womb of royal kings, this England'

No! Not the words of myself! Although my style is
very similar, so I can understand you thinking
that. The words everybody of Sir William
Shakespeare the Bard on Avon, from Othello's
speech to Titania from the Winter's Tale of Loves
Labour's Lost, part two and possibly three.

Now there's a lot of nonsense talked about
Shakespeare, and in this chapter I want to dispel
some of those myths and to a degree de-mystify
the bard. Because I think he has been misted up
by people over the years.

[234]

I am on a mission to make Shakespeare more accessible. People who are doing an O'level might find this chapter particularly useful, and you're probably right in thinking that this book should be a syllabub text book and bought by every school in the country as a teaching aid. Which I am prepared to negotiate on the price, if anyone would like to approach me about that? Like the idiot Michael Grove for instance. Who I can't bring myself to look at. But that wouldn't stop me doing business with him. I'd sell him a few hundred thousand copies of my memoirs.

He could wear a balaclava. You don't have to look at someone to sell them something do you? That's one of the good things about me, it doesn't matter how stupid someone is, or how much he irritates me when he opens his mouth, I will still do business with them, for the good of our children. There might be an order form in this book? I'll see if I can get one put at the back of it. *Need order form.*

So who, or what, was, or is Shakespeare? Well Shakespeare was a man, just like you or me, or I, who wrote plays many, many years ago when everybody talked like Stanley Unwin. This sometimes makes them difficult to follow, but if you follow the following, you will find what I tell you makes it all much easier to follow.

Now, I'm going to take you through a Shakespeare speech, line by line, until I get fed up of it, and tell you what each line means. It's a speech from Hamnet, who was also in the Micky Spillane books.

'OH THAT THIS TO, TO SOLID FLESH'
This means he's fat, 'solid flesh'= fat

'SHOULD MELT, THAW AND RESOLVE ITSELF INTO A DEW'
This is Hamnet saying he'd like to lose weight and I think something about water retention?

"OR THAT THE EVERLASTING HAD NOT FIXED HIS CANNON 'GAINST SELF SLAUGHTER'
Well we all know what a cannon is, so I won't insult you by doing that one. It's fair to assume that, 'The Everlasting' will be God.

'HOW WEARY, STALE, FLAT AND UNPROFITABLE SEEM TO ME ALL THE USES OF THIS WORLD'
Self explanatory.

'OH GOD, OH GOD'
Well that just means, Oh God, Oh, God

That's as much as I'm doing now, for the time being. It is very demanding, translating from Shakespearian. I don't think you understand how much it takes out of you reading all that gobbledy-gook, and the cricket's about to start.

74 for 3. Pieterson out for a duck.

Now when you go to see a Shakespeare, if you find there's a bit you don't understand, and let's face it, that's most of the bloody thing if you're being honest, in those circumstances just copy what the rest of the audience is doing and you'll probably get away with it. Always presuming you haven't nodded off. I'm terrible like that really, me. If I ever get free tickets to see a Shakespeare I always have to have a little nap. Honestly my eyes just start closing. It's not my fault. There's something mesmeric about them droning on. If you're ever having trouble sleeping, that's what you want to do. Get a ticket for 'Midsummers Nights Dreams'.

Possible cure for insomnia?
Or large scotch.

[237]

FLUFFY THE TORTOISE SHELL CAT

A BOOK FOR SMALL CHILDREN TO BUY

BY
COUNT ARTHUR STRONG

Fluffy was a tortoise cat

Fluffy was a tortoise shell cat.

Fluffy was a tortoise-shell cat

Fluffy was a grey cat who could talk. Nobody knew it could talk but Walter, the son of the family. Fluffy was a magic cat. It would only talk to him. No it was a flying cat.

Fluffy was a flying cat with a secret. It could fly!

Fluffy was a cat with a secret. It could fly! One day

Right this next one is it.

Fluffy was a cat, like no other cat with a secret, it could fly an aeroplane. It saved a magic elf it met in the woods stuck in a man

trap, and something about the pot of gold at the
end of the rainbow? And it gave him or her three
wishes. The elf did. The elf gave the cat three
wishes. It's owner (the cats owner, not the
elf) was a young boy called, possibly, Walter?
Possibly Walter was a wizard, a bit like Harry
Potter but with square glasses and blonder and
taller.

One day the cat was walking down the garden
path, considerately resisting the temptation to
do a mess on it, which sounds a bit far fetched
I know! But you have to remember boys and girls,
Fluffy was a magic cat. If only all cats could
do that. The world would be a much nicer place.
People never pick cats mess up do they? I've
never seen anyone pooper scooping after a cat.
You have a look next time you're at the park
children. That can be a project for you.

Fluffy was sitting in the sun licking all it's
fur nice and clean. Don't worry boys and girls,
if any hairs get in the cats throat, the cat
will sick them all up later. Probably on the
settee.

[239]

Anyway a duck called Richard waddled down the
path, because they were near a lake, weren't
they.

"Hello Richard Duck. How are you today", uttered
Fluffy.

"It's my birthday", returned Richard, "Do you
want to come to my party?"

"Yes please", said Fluffy Duck.

"It's at half past two", and it waddled off back
where it came from.

"A party! How exciting. Oh that means I'll have
to get a present", said the cat. To itself.
Obviously.

The cat went home and got it's money box which
was locked so it got a knife and stuck it in the
slot and jiggled it about until enough money
fell out to buy Walter Duck a present. Like a
comb or something that was useful.

So the cat went to the shop. And the shopkeeper
was a friendly elephant called Mr Jumbo.

"Good morning, Fluffy Cat. How are you today?"
Said Mr Jumbo, jollily.

[240]

"I'm very well Mr Jumbo, thank you for
bothering. I've come to buy a birthday present
for whatever the duck's called", purred Fluffy.
"What can I buy for a shiny new 20 pence bit?

"Why twenty pence will buy you this apple,
young man or woman cat. But I must warn you
this is a magic apple and with it you get three
wishes. And with these three wishes comes great
responsibility".

"I'll take it", uttered the fish. Cat. Fluffy
Cat.

So anyway the cat goes back to where it lived.
And it put the apple down on the kitchen table
while it went to the lavatory.

And a wicked fairy godmother looked through the
window and saw the juicy apple on the table and
she said. 'Apple green, Apple red, Come to me,
I must be fed'. And she smashed a window with
a brick and broke into the house and stole the
apple.

When the cat got back from the toilet, were it
had licked its paws thoroughly, like a good cat.
And you must always lick your paws when you've

done the toilet children. It looked at the empty table and saw that it was empty. And it thought, "What have I done with that bloody apple then?". And it mewed loudly, like you hear tom cats do at half past three in the morning, when next doors cat's on heat.

Hearing this plaintiff mew, Walter who'd been playing with his magic wand, in the drawing room, hurried into in to in too into the kitchen to see what was going on.

"What's going on? What are you mewing at?"

And the cat told Walter everything that had happened and Walter looked at his crystal balls and saw that the wicked witch was outside just about to fly off on her broomstick. Quick as a flash he got a passing woodcutter to chop her in two and lo and behold Robin Hood's grandma jumped out, and the cow jumped over the moon.

THE END

CHAPTER 57

THE WILD ONES

In the late 1980's it wasn't only America's Marlbro Brandon that was rebelling. Over this side of the pond we had some of that going on here as well.

I was going through a difficult patch myself, and I take no pride in saying this, for a time, I turned my back on variety and became a junivile delinquent and Teddy Boy. Hang about, this was the 1950s, not the 1980s. Sod it, you sort that out.

The late 50's to me were what I call my 'wildebeast years'. Wilderness years' TIPPEX!!! PLEASE!!! SOMETIME THIS YEAR!!!!

I USED TO HANG AROU

I used to hang around street corners, chewing chewing gum with my mouth open and I was cheeky to my mother. On one occasion I spat at a fly, just for kicks. It was clear to everyone who loved me that I was going right off the rails.

[243]

I remember when Bill Halley's Comet came to Streatham Odeon. I went to see them play with some of the guys, and when they did the song, 'Blackboard Jungle', well the place went wild and we started throwing seats at each other. It was crazy man. Just plain crazy. It's a wonder someone wasn't seriously killed.

Next thing we knew the police or 'pigs' were there, scuffles broke out and I was arrested. I tried to tell them that it was someone else's fault, but they weren't listening. They'd already made their minds up and threw me in the cells.

I felt just about as low as a man could get. I remember a prison officer bringing me my chow. As he went to hand the tray to me he said, "Wait a minute, don't I recognise you?".

I said, "Obviously not daddio, if you have to ask me".

"You're that kid who was doing that show at the Brixton Hippodrome. What the hell happened to you kid?".

'What the hell happened to me kid?' That phrase rang in my ears, like a big bell, ringing. In

my ears. I wished somebody would make it stop.
I slumped in the corner, moodily, a bit like
Montgomery Clift would, and prayed that no
one would try to molest me, because mother had
often said that I was a pretty boy and you hear
stories about what goes on.

In the morning they came for me and took me
to the courthouse. Ma was there holding a
handkerchief up to her head. She was blowing
her nose loudly. It sounded like she had a kazoo
stuck up each nose hole. I couldn't bring myself
to look at her. The Judge read me the riot act
and I was found guilty of what I did last night.
Everything went blurred, I wanted to shout out
but I couldn't speak. Through this sort of kind of
fugg I heard the Judge pass sentence. I was to be
sent to borstal.

socks

CHAPTER 58

BORSTAL

Yes that's right. I said Borstal!

The prison van roared to a halt. The reinforced steel doors were thrown open and I was roughly manhandled out of them. I stood there for a moment letting my eyes become accustomed to the bright sunshine. Somebody shouted at us to line up.

The prison Govenor or 'Guv' as we were not allowed to call him, slowly walked along the line, hands behind his back, fixing each of us with a meaningful glare, almost daring us to step out of line.

After what seemed an eternity, but was probably about 10 to 15 seconds I would estimate, he stopped and addressed us.

"Now I run a tight ship here. If you keep your noses down and do as you're told you'll do alright. If you don't I will crush you. Do I make myself clear? Do I make myself clear"? He said, again, because no one answered him the first time. It's better on film, that sort of thing.

"Yes sir.", we responded. In unison.

"Good", he opined, "Make sure it stays that way. I'll leave you in the capable hands of Officer Campling. Carry on Campling. And with that, Michael Redgrave nodded and wal

And with that he nodded and walked away.

Campling eyed us hungrily. He was, it turned out, a baddie, and he was enjoying his moment. "Look at you miserable lot. You all look as if you could do with a haircut each. Let's see what we can do about that. Left turn quick march".

And with that we were all taken off to have our heads cut off. Most of us HAIR CUT OFF!

And with that we were all taken to have our hair cut off.

Most of us were Teddy Boys, although there was one 'Beatnik' among our number, who was doing time for being 'caught with a dope, smoking'.

[247]

Anyway, us Teddy boys had spent a lot of time perfecting our D A's. Which stands for 'Duck's Arses'. I used to think it stood for 'District Attorney', but apparently it is 'Duck's Arses'. It would be much better if I'd have been right about that. Imagine the confusion a D A, (District Attorney), with a D A, (Duck's Arse), could cause? For example:

"Hello I'm a D A".

"Hello. Nice D A"

"Are you trying to be funny?"

"No"

"Then stop saying stupid things then".

"I'm not saying stupid things".

"You are".

You see what I mean? Neither of me has any idea what the other one's on about. So that needs looking at.

Anyway whatever, they took us to the prison

barber and we all had our hair cut very short. Like they used to do if you had nits.

Of course I never had nits myself. Mother said
that's what common people got and that it was
because my hair was so very fine. Too fine for
the nits to cling on to I would imagine she
meant? I can't think what else she'd have meant.
Perhaps she was drunk? Who knows? Anyway I was
locked up in the hokey for the night.

In the morning we were given vests and baggy
shorts and made to run around a big field. I had
been something of a cross country runner on the
outside and to me this wasn't a punishment. I ran
and ran like the wind and the wind, leaving the
rest of the boys in my wake.

When we finished, Campling, who had it in for me,
told me the Govenor wanted to see me. Apparently
he'd been watching me run (the Govenor, not
Campling), and was rather impressed. I knocked on
his door.

"Come in Courteney", he sai

"Come in Strong", he said. I came in.

"You wanted to see me sir?," I said.

"Do you know what this is Courtn STRONG!" He
handed me a photograph of someone holding a

[249]

I've told you! get Tippex

trophy. (It was a cup actually, but if I'd just said cup you'd have thought it was a picture of somebody just holding a cup. Like a tea cup. That's always a difficult one to do as a writer that. Cup and cup. But good writers can always find a way round it, like I did, can't we?)

"No sir", I replied eventually, after I'd written that bit.

"That is a picture of a posh private school, who we do cross country against every year and they always beat us and win the cup, or trophy as some writers might call it for clarification".

"Thank you for telling me sir", I responded. "Can I go now?"

"No. I haven't told you the rest of the film yet. I was watching you run and I think you have the beating of them. I want you to represent the borstal in next weeks sports day against them".

I thought for a moment and then I spoke for a moment. "I'd rather not sir if it's all the same to you".

He looked at me and his eyes narrowed, and they were already quite narrow to start with.

"I don't think you understand," he proffered, "I can make things very difficult for you here at Ruxton Towers"

"Alright I'll do it then".

For the remainder of the week, I was excused normal duties and allowed to practise running, until the day of the event was upon me. I remember I awoke early and went to give a bit of bacon rind to my kestrel.

When I got to the shed, the kestrel was just lying there on the floor motionless. I knew enough about kestrels to know that they didn't do that. It was dead of a broken neck. I cried until I thought my heart would break. Just then I heard the noise of a branch snapping as someone trod on it behind me. I turned around. It was Crampling, who had it in for me.

"That's a shame Casper", he said mockingly. "You better get yourself ready for the race".

I held back the tears and gritted my jaw. I would get even with them. I'd make them pay for killing my kestrel bird.

We lined up for the race and the starter fired
the staring pistol. The posh ones tried to elbow
me and trip me up but I forced my way to the
front and I opened up an substantial lead.
As I ran into the home straight I could see
the winning tape in front of me. The Michael
Redgrave was standing there willing me on. I
could almost hear him. "Come on, come on", I almost
heard.

Suddenly, quite deliberately I started stopping,
slowly.

"What are you doing you fool? What are you
doing", I almost could hear the Guv say.

I had slowed to a walk by now. I could see
the others gaining on me with every stride.
Do you know, I'll never forget the look of
incredulousness on their faces as they overtook
me.

You know, I think that this would be a much
better film if I won the race. It's not a very
satisfying end, just stopping. It's stupid. So I
think I might start running again and I did and
I overtook all the people that had just overtaken

me, and they all looked incredulous. And I did win the race. And everyone was cheering me on and I had it very easy for the rest of borstal and then when I came out I was in Chariots of Fire and I won that as well. And if you want the truth I'm rushing this now because writing this has made me late for an audition for chewing gum which I have to learn a line for. "This is nice chewing gum". I'll have to learn that on the bus now.

CHAPTER

ANYONE FOR TENNIS (THIS COULD BE IN THE 50s OR THE
80s, IT DOESN'T AFFECT ME)

Now it's widely known that I am a natural
sportsman with great ball sense. If I hadn't gone
on to become what I am, I could have pursued a
distinguished sporting career. It was tennis
that I excelled in. And if I have a regret in
life, which I don't, it was that I didn't turn
professional and win Wimbledon.

I instead, distinguished myself in the Equity
Mixed Doubles.

For those of you who don't know what 'Equity' is,
it is the actors union and everyone used to have
to be in Equity. All of them were in it. Lawrence
Olivier, Dora Bryan, the lot. And once a year they
used to have a tennis tournament.

One morning, on hearing the rattle of the
letterbox rattling, I arose from bed and went
to the door to find the postman forcing a gold

[254]

embossed envelope bearing the Equity's coat of
arms through the door. Obviously not 'through'
the door. Through the letterbox. I remember
thinking it was another bloody reminder about
my subs being in arrears.

On opening the envelope however, I was highly
delighted to find, that inside was something
else. It was a 'wildcard' invitation to take part
in that years Equity Mixed Doubles Tennis
Tournament.

I don't mind telling you I was thrilled. The only
question was who would partner me and where was
my tennis bat?

I knew Dora Bryan was doing a 'Carry On', so that
ruled her out. And then it came to me. Of course!
Why didn't I think of that a minute ago, Anita!
Anita Harris.

I called her immediately and she said she'd
be highly delighted to partner me. She'd just
finished doing a bit on, 'It's Lulu', on the BBBC
and to use her own words she, 'was looking for a
distraction'. I said to her, "Can I just stop you
there Anita?" I said, "If you're partnering me in

this tournament, we're in it to win it." I said, "This might be a distraction to you but I want to use this opportunity to show I could have won Wimbledon. Are you with me! I said, Are you with me!"

"Yes", she said, "Yes!", her eyes shining brightly, like two 100 watt light bulbs. And then we high fived each other, like they do on 'The Voice'. Once again my motivational skills had come to the fore. Now the only thing I had to do was find my lucky racquet.

I called it my 'lucky' racquet because I'd found it in a bus shelter. And I know it was silly of me but I was quite superstitious about playing with it. It was a real beauty. Wooden framed, like they used to be, and strung with cat gut.

I would estimate there was the guts of at least two or possibly three cats went into stringing that racquet, which I always found strangely reassuring. I'd won quite a few matches with that in my youth. The 'lob' shot being one of my favourite shots. People would come from miles to see me lobbing it off the old cat's guts.

I spent the next few weeks bringing myself to the peak of physical condition. I would start each day with 15 minutes of Canadian Mountie exercises, then have a banana and then look for my racquet for a bit. Pretty soon I was match ready. Then on the eve of the match right out of the blue, like a bouncing bomb on a Norwegian fiord, Anita dropped the bombshell she dropped on me.

The telephone rang, just like it had on many, many occasions before and in keeping with that statement I answered it in the same vein. "Helleo, Tooting 2469, Count Arthur Strong speaking. How may I help you?'

"It's Anita", Anita's voice said to me. She sounded slightly querulous in tone and I notice this, so I said, "Why do you sound slightly querulous in tone Anita?

"Oh Arthur, I don't know how to tell you" she sobbed.

"Tell me? Tell me what my dear. Come, come it can't be as bad as all that can it? Just take your courage in both hands and tell me. After all they do say a problem shared is a problem doubled or halved, I forget which".

She then went on to drop the bombshell that she couldn't partner me in the Equity Mixed Doubles after all. She'd been offered an engagement with Vince Hill on the Queen Mary and was setting sail that night. Vince had just had a version of 'Edelweiss' in the hit parade twenty years earlier and his popularity was at an all time high. For five minutes. But not to worry, she said she'd already spoken to Hattie Jaques and that Hattie was free to partner me.

"Hattie Jaques! Hattie Jaques!" I exclaimed "Tennis! Hattie Jaques! How's she going to get round a tennis court?

"She's good at net" Anita responded.

"Well I hope we're playing against Mrs Mills and Fred Emney, that's all I can say. You've let me down Anita! You've let me down!"

The morning of the match was upon me. I starched and pressed my shorts and tennis skirt and set off for Queens. The morning sky was overcast, almost brooding. Was that a spot of rain I felt

[258]

on the back of my wrist? The beginnings of an
idea began to form within my head of mine.

As I arrived at Wimbledon, I felt more spots
on the back of my wrist (ditto). I hoped I
wasn't coming down with something. The massed
spectators we're sitting there expectantly. Hattie
was pacing the corridor, which I always think
looks Spanish. Matador. "What's up with you?", I
said nicely.

"Nothing", she said.

"Where's your racquet", I enquired.

"What racquet?"

"Your racquet!" She looked at me as though I was
a complete idiot, which I'm not. "The thing you hit
the ball with! A racquet!

"No one told me to bring a racquet", she said
defensively.

"You shouldn't need telling", I shouted, still
nicely.

"Well where's yours then?" She said.

corridor
matador
torneodor
stevedor ?

cabbage
Liver
1 Onion
toilet paper
air freshner

I looked down at my hand where my cats gut racquet should be, but it was empty of it. I had left it on the bus. And that 31 would be at the terminus in Camden Town by now, approximately six miles away, or it might be further.

Things were going from bad to worser. How could we play tennis without a racquet between us each? But wait, just at that precise moment I started to be hit on the head by lots of plops and the plops were getting heavier. It was raining. Torrentially!

The umpire in his chair leant down toward me, "What are we going to do? We can't play in this rain. We've only got the court booked for an hour. They'll want another pound. We'll have to abandon the tournament."

I could see he was becoming hysterical so I slapped him in the face until he shut up then I leapt into acton and I grabbed the microphone from him.

"Ladies and gentlemen! Stay right where you are. In my business we have a little saying, 'The show must go on'." And I got up in the audience and started singing to them all for ages. Like Cliff Richards did but better and I did it first. And it was marvellous. They all said that.

And afterwards one of the locals, Barnsley Bob, who was watching from the other side of the wire netting, banging a dustbin lid to accompany me, gave me a can of something called 'Special Brew' and we adjourned to a park bench and I sang a few more songs with some of his friends. And it really was an unforgettable show. It was just my bad luck there weren't any television cameras there. He's a jammy sod, Cliff Richards.

CHAPTER

THE ENTERTAINMENT GAME

NOW WHAT YOU MIGHT   SEE! BLOODY STUCK
AGAINAGAIN!

It would be a lot better if you would have just
let me write the whole bloody book in capitals
like I said. I really am tremendously fed up
with you about that. I can't overestimate or
underestimate how much. It all takes twice as
long like this. I'm already into the third week
on this book! When I do the next volume, and I'm
not arguing with you, even if I have to go to the
top of Faber and Faber and Faber, I'm going to do
it my way, ALL CAPITALS. I bet I'd be able to get it
down to two weeks if I did. Then we can see which
one sells best, and whichever one it is, I'll use
for the third volume. Right!

CHAPTER

THE ENTERTAINMENT GAME

Now what you might not know about me is
that as well as all the other things I am,
I am also an inventor and entrepeneur.
entrepenure entrepenur. And actually I have
probably invented several things you use in
your everyday life. Unfortunately though I
can't currently tell you what they are or say
anything about them because of several patent
issues with small minded companies.

what's a Venture Capitalist

But one of the things I have invented which
I had a lot of fun with is my entertainment
based board game called, 'The Entertainment
Game'(TM). And this will be coming out hopefully
for Christmas. If we can't get it out in time for
Christmas, we might hold it back for Easter.
Whenever that is.

That should be a board game itself, 'When Is
Easter'. I don't know why it can't be the same time
every year? Apparently it's the first Sunday,

after the first full moon after the venereal
equinox. Which is also the first day of spring.
And that is, when day and night are both 12
hours long. Marvellous isn't it? And every year
they expect us to do all that for them. Instead
of just saying, 'It's on the so and so of so and
so every year'. Which would be much simpler. Who
decides these things?   ———   *Alan*
                                        Saga

Anyway what you do to play The Entertainment
Game (TM) is: on the board, you, (there's a board,
obviously), on the board, it looks like a
Monopoly board a bit, but it definitely isn't
Monopoly. It's quite definitely not that, so don't
even think it is. Right I'm going to start this
bit again.

What you do to play the Entertainment Game
(TM) is, there's a board, and on that board there
are theatres where there would be streets on a
Monopoly board, and that is completely different,
if you're Trades and Standards people reading
this. Streets and theatres are not similar. One's
inside and one's outside for a start. And you
have dice or dices because there's two of them. No
three of them! Because that's even more different

3.10
Kempton
apple tree
£1 e.w.

to Monopoly. They only have two, because it's
cheap.

Now you throw the dices, and you have counters
you move along. And the counters are shaped like
awards. One is an 'Oscar'. And one is a 'Bafta'. And
one is a 'TV Quick' award, and one is a 'British
Soap Awards' thing, if they have one, and for the
others I might have an ironing board and hat if
there aren't any more awards. But not a top hat
like bloody Monopoly has. A trilby. A proper hat
like mine. And the dog would be a Bloodhound or
something not a Highland thing, yapping all the
time. And each player has some money, but more
than you get in Monopoly.

And what you do is, you roll the dices and
whoever gets a six goes first and if you land
on a theatre you can buy it and if anybody else
lands on it once you own it they have to pay
you for a ticket to see the show. And you have
squares that you land on that that you have
to pick a card up. One is 'Auditions' and the
other is 'Reviews'. And the reviews one might say,
'Four Star review for your Bottom in Midsummer
Night's Murders. Go forward three spaces'. And

Sooty is a puppet.

you go forward three spaces. And an 'Audition' one might say, 'Up for the part of James Bond in 'Goldenfinger with Love'. Say something like James Bond would. But not when Roger Moore doing it'.

And instead of 'Free Parking' I'd have 'The Interval'.

And instead of mortgaging properties, like that other game, that I'm sick of saying the name of does, The theatre goes 'Dark'. Which is a theatrical expression for when the Arts Council withdraws funding and you can't afford to open except for Derren Brown's shows. And a lot of other stuff I can't be bothered with.

Anyway the point of the game is to buy all the theatres up and win all the money. Then if you own all the theatres you can put what you like on, and play all the good parts, instead of scratching around waiting for some half wit to say you can push a trolley past the bottom of a corridor. And it's nothing like Monopoly.

Stamp

CHAPTER 60

DOWN AND OUT IN FRANCE AND BOULOGNE

One of the things with being a highly
recognisable celebrity like me, is that you're
never off duty. Even if you're just going to the
shop for a loaf of bread, or an orange, someone's
going to recognise you and want to speak to you,
so to speak.

We've all heard of 'Beatlemania' haven't we? Well
you know 'Beatlemania' didn't start with The
Beatles, as they would have you believe. I had
'Beatlemania' happening to me long before they
came along.

I once remember going to the greengrocer and
being followed home by an ardent fan. I had to
push him a banana through the letterbox before
he went away. Finally though he did. *restraining order*

Anyway things reached a peak for me in 1960
something. I was recognised three times in one
week. Someone that lived in my street said hello. *Mrs Kay?*

Someone I was briefly at school with nodded at me as they were walking past, I think it was me they were nodding at, and the woman in the bank asked how I was. Life was becoming intolerable.

I decide that the only thing for it, was to remove myself from the merry go round of constant recognition and take a bit of time out before I broke down and had a breakdown. It was time to get back to myself and find me.

I decided to buy a map of Europe, open it out on the kitchen table, close my eyes and stick a pin in it. Wheresoever that pin wouldst falleth wouldst be wherever I wents to.

The first time I tried it, I unfortunately missed the table, which could have been nasty. However, with nothing more than my pride wounded I tried again. This time, I stuck the pin in my leg, which was nasty. It was a big pin. But I was getting close to the map with every attempt. The third I stuck it in the middle of the North Sea, and I wasn't about to go there. For a kick off I didn't have a boat and there's a lot of water there. But with the famous Count Arthur Strong ne-er say die attitude, that's got me where I am today, it was fourth time lucky, and with a trembling something, I looked down at the map to see where fate had dictated I go to.

It was Boulogne! In France. Oh Boulogne! The very name conjured up a hundred images in my mind of mine.

France, the country of Mireille Matieu, Sacha Distel, Edam cheese, wine of every hue and colour. Spaghetti, Papa and Nichole off the Renault and cold soup!

I was doing just what William the Conqueror had done thousands of years before me, but the other way round, I was going to France.

The very next day, or the day after, I forget which, I went down to Thomas Cookes's and booked passage on a cross channel ferry. I decided as I was escaping my celebrity, to travel incognito as a poor man, out to make his way in the new world of Europe. So I travelled steerage and was given a berth in the bowels of the ship, next to the engine room. I remember leaning against the railings, or whatever they call them on a boat, as the ship pulled out of the port of Dover, and thinking what will become of me in this brave new world? I breathed a deep lung full of the ozone, but not enough to make the hole any bigger, I was very careful about that, before you start complaining, and headed downstairs. There is a word for downstairs on a boat, I just can't remember it. No! It's gone.

I'd never slept in a hammock before. In fact when the purser said it to me, I though he'd said 'a haddock'. Which would have been ludicrous, as I told him at the time. In fact, I suggested they changed the name of them to avoid any confusion in the future. Someone that wasn't as clever as me at thinking things out, might be very upset about the notion of having to sleep on a haddock. A pregnant woman for instance. That would be a genuine ordeal for someone like that. And not everybody likes fish. But he was a surly individual and I could see that my advice had fell on stony ground.

During my passage I decided to keep myself to myself. If word got out that I was on board my journey would have become intolerable. So I kept my head down and spent most of my time in my

[270]

haddo
cod
bass
mac
plai
eel
sea
ho
dolp
flou
Ang
fi
chut
Octopus!

haddock reading a book. A week later we arrived at Boulogne.

I'll never forget sailing into the harbour at Boulogne, which apparently is pronounced 'Boo-Loin' and not 'Boo-log-knee' as I'd been saying it. There are a lot of French words like that. It's like a foreign language.

I disembarked and got off the ship. I remember standing on the jetty and thinking, here I was at last. Somewhere where nobody knew me. Somewhere where where I didn't have to be 'Count' Arthur Strong, I could just be plain old Arthur Strong.

I have to say, my next thought was, 'Why would anyone want to be somewhere, where nobody knew who you were?' That's a death knell to a celebrity like me. I might as well be Barrymore! Once I'd realised the error of my ways I thought, 'Right I've seen France. Very nice.' I then bought 14 carte postals, as they're called over there, I wrote a few, 'Wish I was there's' on them, stuck them in a post box and got back on the ship.

I booked a nice cabin on the way back as well. With a proper bed. I thought I'm not sleeping in a bloody haddock with the great unwashed for another week. *no offence* .

I booked my return passage without subterfuge, and of course because of that, I was invited to dine every night with the ships Captain at the top table.

My pilgrimage to Boulogne had taught me something. And it was not to turn my back on myself. Like the Queen, I was duty bound to play with the hand that fate had dealt me. Whatever the pressures.

Those twelve minutes in France had reinvigorated me and I've been there for twelve minutes many times since. Anyway here I was back from my travels, and I was ready. Ready for anything.

By the way they've stopped asking at the tills in W H Smiths if you 'want any of our half price sweets and chocolate'. They now say, 'Would you like any of our offers?' There trying to come at you from another direction. They must think I was born yesterday.

Mind you, two big bars of Galaxy for three pounds is quite a good offer. I can easily go

Make pills

through a whole bar at one sitting me. If I'm
concentrating on something else. I ate half of
one during Coronation Street on Monday and I'll
be eating the other half during Wednesdays, if
I know me, which I do. So you know, whilst I can
appreciate a good offer as well as the man stood
next to the man stood next to me can, I don't have
to agree with the methods they employ. And I
don't. They should shut up when they talk to me
and just have a sign up. They've even started in
the bloody post office now. She said to me this
morning, "Can I get you any stamps or provide you
with any of our other services today?"

I said, "No. You can't. And stop asking me. I know
what you're doing you know. You're as bad as the
woman in Smith's! This is the post office! This is
one of the last bastions is this!"

I'm just going to write down here, now, for all
you fans of mine that are reading this book, that
work in W H Smiths or the bloody Post Office. Do
not, I repeat repeat not, ask me if I want things
when I come in your shops. There isn't the time in
the day for you to be asking me if I want things.
I'm a busy man, I've got this book to write.

Stamps!!

In fact this book is the only thing I could think of that would be valid for you to ask people if they want, when they're standing at the tills. So the one exemption to what I'm saying is, that you could ask everybody but me if they want this book. When I've finished it obviously.

Do not. I repeat. Do not, for God's sake start asking me if I want my own book. That would be the straw that broke the camels back off. Faber and Faber and Faber have said they'll send me a box full of the things. They better do. The bloody work I've put into this. Books don't make themselves up you know. Anyway either buy this or put it down now. You've been looking at it for long enough.

CHAPTER 63

DES O'CONNOR

Des O'Connor was

no he wasn't.
He liked to think
he was!

CHHAPTER 64

LORD BADEN POWELL

AND

THE SCOUTING MOVEMENT

The scouting movement is something that has always been very important to me. And I have been involved in it all my life. And yes, I myself was a Boy Scout which I didn't mention earlier, not because I'd forgotten, but because I've just thought of it.

So before I carry on, let me fill you in on some of the background of this wonderful and erstwhile organisation.

Lord Baden Powell was the founder of the scouting movement. In many ways it can be said, without fear of contradiction that he was indeed, the first boy scout. In fact the Hollywood star, Harrison George, based Indiana Jones on him in the Lord of the Rings films, and he wrote Peter Pan. Lord Baden Baden did. Not George Harrison.

[276]

George Harrison was one of the Beatles. *the drummer*

In 1900 and something, the story goes, Lord Baden
Baden was sitting at his desk looking out of his
window and he saw two youths leaning against
a bus stop with their hands in their pockets.
When he went to bed that night he dreamed that
he heard a voice, and that voice was someone
telling him to invent the boy scouts. When he
woke up in the morning he sat at his desk and
with a pencil in his hand, and feverishly mapped
out the boy scouts charter. 'Job a Bob', the two
fingered salute, badges, saying 'Dib dib dib',
singing Ging gang goolies, the lot. Thus was laid
the foundation stone of the boy scouts.

But he still needed Royal dissent. So because
he was a Lord he phoned up Buckingham Palace,
all the Lords have a direct line through to the
Queen, it dates back to the Knights of the Round
Table, and got he got the seal of Royal approval,
and the rest is history.

Little did Lord Baden Harrison imagine that
hundreds of years later the Boy Scouts would
still be going and I would have become an *guitarist.*
dispensable part of it all.

[277]

In 1970 something, I remember vividly, there was a knock at my door. On opening it I was delighted to see the vicar stood there, looking at me.

"Count Arthur," he said, "I'd like to ask something of you because of all your expertise".

"Well you better sit down Vicar, while I pour the tea", I ejaculated to him.

"Can I come in the house then?" he enquired politely.

"Of course! What must you think of me?" I laughed out loud. I've always been able to laugh at myself. It's one of the good things about someone like me. Or me. *Me*

I asked him in for tea and cake, if he'd brought one, and this is what he said to me.

"Count Arthur, I'm afraid I'm here to ask you a favour".

" Well you mustn't be afraid to ask me a favour Vicar, I don't bite you know," I joked. "And even if I did, I would only do it in self defence, and you'd have had to seriously provoke me for it to go that far. So you'd only have yourself to blame should that scenario occur."

He looked at me with great understanding in his eyes before he went on thus, "I'm afraid it's the Scouts Hut".

"You're afraid what's the Scouts Hut?" I said quizzically, not fully understanding the thing he'd just said to me. (Don't worry. I think it'll become clearer).

"Perhaps if you'd let me finish?", he intoned.

"Yes I think you should", I responded, "But first let me say this to you. You're among friends in this house Vicar, never forget that. If you're afraid of the Scouts Hut we'll get you through it."

Once again he gave me that look and I felt we'd somehow connected on a deep and meaningful level.

"Look", he said, putting his hand over my mouth, which he sometimes did.

"Look", he said, "the Scout's Hut will fall down if we don't raise some money for a new roof. Because of who you are and as an ex boy scout yourself of some not inconsiderable distinction, I am here to ask you if you can think of any way we can raise the necessary funds to replace the roof I've just mentioned earlier in this speech?"

With that, he removed his hand and I was once again free to commune with him. Or in fact use my mouth for any purpose I wanted, without recrimination. After all we lived in a democracy last time I looked.

As it happened I couldn't really think of anything else to do with it but speak, so I did.

"You've come to the right house Vicar", I exclaimed, with fire in my eyes. "Vicar, an idea is beginning to unfold itself in my mind of mine. What if we were to do a Gang Show, Vicar, like they used to do? I would direct of course, like Ralph Reader, and possibly star, we'll not fall out over that, and I could get some of my showbiz pals to donate their services for naught. By hook or by crook Vicar thou shalt havest thy new shed roof".

The next few weeks went by in what seemed like just a few weeks, so busy was I. After the Vicar's departure, I had wasted no time in contacting some of my old showbiz chums and I spent many

[280]

Stan Stennet

Ken Platt.

days in anticipation of the postman coming,
sticking their replies through my letterbox.
All crumpled up and folded in half, because of
a personal vendetta he was pursuing against
me. Which actually was a tragic accident that
went terribly wrong. I was more a bystander, if
anything.

It was meant to give a cat an electric shock,
not a human being. How was I to know the
idiot postman was going to waltz up the path
unannounced, with letters for me? Wearing steel
toe caps! They should let you know they're coming.
That is a gross dereliction of duty. As I told
him, when we were waiting for the ambulance to
come. It was only connected up to a car battery
anyway. That's not going to kill you is it?

I said, "If you'd had the right shoes on, you
probably wouldn't have felt anything. How can
you having the wrong shoes on be my fault. It
was an 'act of God' you walking up the path when
I was doing a trial."

Anyway he's been very off with me ever since. It's
laughable how some people can be so petty. He
wants to get over it if you ask me.

It was a good idea that was as well, an electrified cat grid. I still might have a go with that on 'Dragon's Den'. He's probably cost me a fortune that idiot.

I think out of them all, I'd have to go with Peter Jones's offer. I think he would have see the merit in my flap. And he knows a lot about the BT side of things, he's always saying. Whatever that means. He makes it sound as if it's a plus.

I wouldn't go with Theo Pafitis, because he just has a stationers shop, I think, and I can't see that being the right place to shift electrical cat flaps. Unless it's W H Smiths. They could sell them at the tills then.

"Could I interest you in any of our Electrified Cat Flaps".

I definitely wouldn't go with Duncan Ballantyne, because I can't understand what he's saying, and you can't have a business relationship based on incoherence.

Anyway, by the end of the week I'd had all the replies to my invitation to all my showbiz pals to participate and my wonderful cast was finalised. They were: Seven scouts, two girl guides, three cubs and topping the bill none other than myself, Count Arthur Strong! What a show this was going to be.

It was decided that the show would open with me singing the big Frankie Vaughn hit, 'Gimmie the Moonlight'. Then I'd say hello to the audience and tell them some jokes for about half an hour. Then I'd do a few magic tricks for a bit. Then I'd sing another song. Then it would be the interval. Then after the interval I'd do another song to open the second half. Then, I'd get someone up from the audience and make a fool of them for a bit, like Bruce Forsyth used to, when he knew where he was. Then I might let the audience ask me a few questions like on 'An Audience with Ken Dodd'. Then I'd do my Memory Man act, which would really bring the house down, and then I'd finish on a song. Probably the theme from 'Minder'. Or something from 'Fiddler on the Roof' Then the other's would come on and do a bow.

As I said to the Vicar, when I was running this by him, if a show like this doesn't get a new roof for the scouts hut, I don't know what will.

[283]

Anyway he said he'd mull it over. I must give him a ring about that actually. Because that was a good few years ago now.

Come to think of it he's not at the church anymore, Father Thompson. I'm sure I remember someone saying he's gone to South Africa.

It was probably the verger, which, as I was telling him, being a verger is a voluntary position. Any idiot can be a verger. Why he has to have a smock I don't know. He's a retired mechanic. If truth be known, I think he's suffering a little bit from what they call 'delusions of grandeur'. Which is just a bit sad if you ask me. What do they say, 'power corrupts'?

CHAPTER

THE PARTY'S OVER

When I finished at Margate that summer, I knew
that something was wrong. Among other things,
I had a ringing in my ears which only stopped
when I answered the telephone. Something had to
be done.

I decided to make an appointment to see a top
Harley Street specialist in the field. I don't
mean I saw him in a field. That would be stupid.
I saw him in Harley Street. Why would anybody
think a top Harley Street specialist would see me
in a field. They wouldn't do that. For a kick off I
would imagine it would be unhygienic to examine
someone's ears in a field. What if there were
sheep in it? Or worse, cows! You could end up with
foot and mouth in your ear.

I would say there's a very good chance that
anyone that says they're a Harley Street
specialist, that suggests examining you in a
field, is a charlatan. They wouldn't fool me for

a minute. A proper one would have a suite of Harley Street consulting rooms, and you could have a coffee and a custard cream while you were waiting, sitting on a faux leather Chesterfield. With a side table, bestrewed with posh magazines. 'Horses and Hounds' and suchlike. 'Houses and Gardens'. 'Gardens and Horses'. Horses and Houses". 'Exchange and Mart'.

And he'd be titled. Sir Roger Manners, for instance would be a good name for one of them. The only field you'd see Sir Roger in would be on a shoot. Bagging some braces of grouses or two. It's a ridiculous notion to even think for a second, that someone like the, admittedly fictional Sir Roger, would ever, ever, examine someone in a field. You're thinking of a vet.

Anyway I ended up going to my G P instead. Because you can't get a Harley Street specialist on the National Health. You have to pay hundreds of pounds to see one, which I think is scandalous. What kind of service is that? They were very off with me when I tried to make an appointment. Stuck up bunch. And they're all titled you know. All 'Lord' this and 'Sir' that.

Anyway, the upshot of my examination was that it was most likely that there was something wrong with my telephone. Not me. So that was a huge relief to myself, and yet again, not for the first time, I had defied the odds again.

CHAPTER 66

THE TELEPHONE RINGETH

Talking of the telephone, in this wonderful game
I'm in, one never know just what waits for one
around one's corner. Those quiet times between
engagements are often exciting times, filled with
anticipation, because you just don't know what
the next offer of work is going to be. And every
time the telephone rings you heater races just *hear*
that bit faster.

I recall one such occasion. It was just after
what happened in the last chapter and I was
recovering at home from the shock of finding
out that there was nothing wrong with me. The G
P O had been and fixed my telephone and Doctor
Bakers diagnosis that, that was the cause of the
intermittent ringing in my ears proved to be
accurate, and it

Suddenly the telephone rang, interrupting me
as I was writing that. I put down the cheap
typewriter that Faber and Faber and Faber had

[288]

'loaned' me, (if you can believe that! Tight sods), and crossed to my chestnut formica'd telephone table, which was the phone's usual resting place.

"Helleo" I spoke, after having first picked up the telephone and placed it against the side of my head. Obviously.

"Do I have the pleasure of speaking to Count Arthur Strong?", it said.

"Why? What's it to you?", I responded, in a slightly guarded way. After all this could have been anyone. I'd had crank calls before. For all I knew this could have been a burglar, casing the joint, or someone trying to miss-sell me insurance, or a stupid yellow nine year old cartoon asking if 'Hugh Jass' is there as I'd seen recently on the television.

"My name is Sir Alex Guinness, and I would like to speak to Count Arthur Strong, if you would convey that message to him I would be most grateful."

"Trying to connect you now caller", I ad-libbed, cleverly buying myself some time to write this next bit.

Alex Guinness. Alex Guinness. It had been a
long time since I'd heard that name and I was
immediately transported back to the last time I'd
seen him. It was in Berwick Street market. I was
buying some fruit and vegetables.

If you got down there towards the end of the day
they did it a bit cheaper for you. Sometimes it
was a lot cheaper, if it was all on the turn. You
could get a whole box of tomatoes for a bob. But
that probably meant that you had to eat them all
before it went off, as soon as you got home. Which
often meant spending most of the following day
or two on the lavatory.

As I looked up from my transaction with a barrow
boy for some of his plums, I spotted Alex over the
other side of the road buying bananas. He didn't
see me and I quickly concealed myself behind a
shop front awning, and waited until he had gone.
I remembered our last meeting, and was in no
hurry to speak with him.

I've never told anyone before the story of
what went on between Alex and myself. Why we
fell out, and actually something is literally
just occurring to me, that I might be able to

make more money out of this if I tell one of
the magazines, rather than write it here. Like
'Hello' or that other one that's always got
bloody Lorraine Kelly on the front, or that
other one that's always got Kerry Katonka on it
saying how she's ballooned up or slimmed down
depending whether she's got a book coming out.
It's ridiculous what some of them will do when
they've got something to promote.

Hey that's not a bad idea actually, if I get this
story in 'Hello' about Alex Guinness taking one
of my shoes, that will be wonderful publicity for
this coming out.

Right well we'll forget this bit then until
I've heard what all the bids are from all the
magazine people.

Dandy
Beano
Topper
Beezer
Hotspur
cheese
milk

CHAPTER

WEIGHT! THERE'S A PROBLEM.

One morning when everything, on the surface, was
going well for me, I looked in the mirror in the
bathroom to see that my weight had ballooned
up. I looked like Michael Ball does these days.
It was because I was unhappy and depressed and
no one understood me. Over a period of time, I had
become addicted to Frey Bentos Steak and Kidney
Puddings, the ones they put in a tin, which I
think is clever. A pudding in a tin. That's what
they call a USP. A unique selling point. Name
another suet based pudding in a tin. You can't.
Alright, they do a treacle pudding in a tin, but
that is a desert isn't it? And it's not suet. It's
pastry. So you're wrong on both counts. *its spong*
isn't it ?
I suppose my binging eating started at

It's not going to work this. It doesn't really
work for a man. It's just not the same when a man
sticks his fingers down his throat.
Its usually because of
[292] *drink with a m*

CHAPTER 67

THE THING ABVOUT ME!

The thing about me is that I never stop thinking
about the next ida

The thing about me is that I never stop thinking
about the next idea. About what tomorrow might
bring. About just what's around the next corner.
I am, to a degree what they call a good old
fashioned 'ideas man'. And I always have been. It's
what get's me out of bed in the morning. That and
needing the toilet. And the water pipes knocking.
Which I will be having seen to. Apparently it's
an airlock. How does the air get in there in the
first place?

I've a good mind to send a letter in to 'The
Unexplained', which is a periodical I subscribe
to, about that. I could also ask them to explain
why it never sodding came this morning. See what
they say about that. Never mind flying saucers
landing in the Grand Canyon and the Ancient
Egyptians coming from Mars. Where's my bloody
'Unexplained' today?

[293]

And you know it's funny where good ideas come from, if I can just bring you back to what I'm talking about. Most of my ideas come to me, in my less guarded moments, shall we say. In the smallest room in the house, to put it delicately, with a toilet in it.

Oh yes, I've had some real crackerjack ideas in the lavatory. I should put a desk in there. I suppose it could be something to do with there always being a plentiful supply of paper to write on. And my particular brand of lavatory paper, (Izal), does lend itself very well to being written on. It makes very good tracing paper as well. Also you can put a sheet of it against a comb and bingo you've got your own kazoo!

And you can still use the Izal for its intended purpose after you've written or kazoo'd on it. It's totally recyclable. So in my own small way, I'm single handedly saving the planet as well.

Some might say, it's a good job that there are people like me around. And that's very nice of them. I couldn't possibly comment. One, (I) does what one, (ditto) can. I neither seek or expect plaudits for my small contribution to the Kohoto

toilet
pap
antisept
cream
grah
bread

Agreement. It's up to other people if they want to nominate me for an OBE, say?

In fact now I think of it there might be a potential sponsorship deal there? With the toilet paper people? I don't think anybody's been hooked up with toilet paper before? I'll look into that. I know Johnny Vegas had 'Hobnobs'. I saw that on a poster. When I first read it I thought it was some kind of medical condition. In fact it was a long time before I could eat one, with that in my head.

I'd make a good ambassador for toilet paper I would. I'm well spoken, always smart and most importantly I use the product. Which would be a real boost to consumer confidence.

See what I mean? I've only been in the lavatory ten minutes with the typewriter on my knee and I've already come up with a bit of business. I wish I'd have thought of bringing the typewriter in here earlier. I'd have finished this bloody book by now.

Anyway I've had a wonderful idea for a book about me. A candid and open account of my life, peppered with wonderful stories about

No I'm doubling up there. That's what this is susposed to be. I thought it sounded familiar. Forget that then.

Alright, here you are, thinking on my feet, how about a radio documentary about me. That would be brilliant. A radio documentary of the book! We could get Mike Yarwood to do impressions of all the famous people I knew. Of course, he'd only do impressions of the truth obviously. That goes without saying. And I would police that most vociferously.

Anyway, we don't need to tell them it's Yarwood. And I'd write what they say, because I know what they said. Of course I'd have to dress it up a bit, because it is for radio. I'll get that on a piece of toilet paper, and I'll send it off to Alan Yentil at BBBC2.

You see what I'm saying about ideas in here? I come to life in the toilet me!

CAHPTER 8

I SEEK TO HELP

Of course in life one, (you), must always think about what one, (you), can give back. And you, (one), can give back in many, many ways. One, (no), of the things that I did in 1960 something was, was, was, I put a card in the post office window advertising 'Acting Classes' at a reduced rate. I thought, what better way is there for me to give something back and spread some of my knowledge base I've accrued over the years, than to encourage an aspiring student or two. And who knew, with my experience and tutelage I might discover the next Audrey Hepworth, or Marlbro Brandon again.

I'll never forget that day I'm about to remember. I was making myself a cup of Typhoo when I heard a little, timid, nervous knock at the door. It sounded like a tiny mouse was tapping on it, with a twig. Or a feather. You decide.

I opened the door. Standing there was a young man. He spoke, but so quietly I couldn't hear the words he utttered.

"Come, come, young fellow! This won't do," I ejaculated. "Take a deep breath and start again".

Little did I know it, but my instruction to take this deep breath he took, was the beginning of a relationship that would propel this young man to stardom. I won't say who he was. See if you can guess.

"Excuse me sir", he responded. "My name is Euan McDonald off 'Trainspotting', although obviously I haven't done that yet. And I came in response to your card in the post office."

Now, I didn't understand a word of that, so strong was his Scottish brogue, but after a series of frantic gesticulations it became apparent to me why he'd turned up on my doorstep. So I brought him a bucket of warm soapy water.

Once he'd finished cleaning my windows, he tapped on the door again, barely as loud as a little sparrow's beak would, if it'd mistaken my door for bread.

I opened the door, "What's that? You've finished my windows have you?"

He shook his head vigorously, until I though it might fall off, such was his passion. He then reached inside his inside pocket and from inside pulled out a card from inside it. It was the card I, myself, had, not two days hence of what I'm saying, placed in the post office window.

He thrust the card before me and pointed with a trembling finger at my words. At once I understood! My card must have somehow fallen down and been wafted out onto the street, and this goodly, honest youth, seeing this was so, had returned it to me. I put my hand in my pocket and pulled out a bright shiny penny piece.

"Take this young man as a reward for your good deed. Today you have truly learned a valuable lesson, honesty is the best policy". And without waiting to be thanked, I pocketed the card and slammed the door quietly shut.

There then followed several more such episodes, but it eventually became apparent that as well as being a window cleaner, a gardener, a plumber, an electrician and returning my post office card to me, he wanted me to give him acting classes.

The next few eeks passed in a haze. I must admit *weeks* there were many times when I though I'd taken too much on. But somehow we got through it and bit by bit, I began to understand what he was saying. It was like Audrey Hepworth's eureka moment in 'Pigsmailion'

Once he'd mastered the English language, there was no stopping him. And eventually I'd taught him as much as I could be bothered to.

I'll never forget the day when he called round to my house to say goodbye.

I was upstairs, dealing with some correspondences I'd had, when suddenly, there was a loud, confident 'rat-a-tat-tat' on my door. It sounded like a bazooka going off. So different to the tentative knockings of several weeks earlier. I walked along my hall, which was fitted with wall to wall 'Axminster' carpet from Cyril Lord's (luxury you can afford), on easy payments, to the front door, passing several of my Capodimonte figurines, which I was an avid collector of.

Along with the 'All-in wrestler, Mick McManus. My favourite one that I had was the one with the two men fishing, and one of them's got his hook caught in the others shirt collar and the dog's got a fish in it's mouth. To me they strike the perfect balance between classical art.

They used to have like a fleur-de-lis mark on them. If you ever see one of those at a car boot, buy it. They're worth a bomb. They're about 400 years old those ones are, you know. My one's I've got are more 1970's, up to today. They just have stickers on them now. I've got about three of them, all in fairly good condition. Just light surface cracks, which you expect, and a broken fishing rod. The dog's only got three legs as well. But you do see three legged dogs sometimes don't you, so I might be able to get away with that? If I ever sell. Crack on it's a three legged sausage dog. Not that I would sell them. I'm what the experts call sentimentally attached to them.

The condition is probably what an expert would call 'Good to fine'. And I didn't pay more than about twenty pence for any of them. They must be worth, well I don't know? I'll have to get an auction house in to value them for insurance purposes. I've only got them on the house insurance and that lapsed ten or fifteen years ago.

I've always thought I'd make a good expert on the Antique Roadshow, me. I could be the ceramics expert, with my vast knowledge. Or I could do watches. I've got about thirty odd watches. Timex, the lot. Oh yes I'm very well know in certain circles for my horological bent.

I'll tell you something though, about 'The Antiques Roadshow', don't you think Hugh Scully looks like a werewolf? I do. You have a look next time he's on. And I tell you something else, you never see him doing it when there's a full moon do you?

It's alright everybody, I'm only joking with you! I know there's no such thing. And even if there was they wouldn't ask a werewolf to do 'Song's of Praise' like he did, would they? Mind you someone would be for the high jump if they did. Heads would roll at the BBBC. If it was true, I expect they'd call that, 'Scullygate?' Or 'Werewolfgate?' Or 'Wolfgate'?

They might call it, 'Songsofpraisegate', but
that's a bit long. Still it's not as long as,
'Hughscullyisawerewolfonsongsofpraisegate', is
it? That would be ridiculous. There are forty
letters in that. I've just counted them. The whole
point of doing a 'somethinggates' is so it's short
and catchy. Not so it gives you jaw ache by the
time you've said it. Like signposts in Wales do.

CHAPTER

I ANGLE

Through my life, whenever I've wanted to get away from it all, I've always found great solace in, 'the sport of Kings'. Fishing.

I'll never forget the first time I went fishing. I didn't catch a fish but I thoroughly enjoyed it. And I'll never forget that. Not catching a fish. I was hooked!

I'm fortunate in that I don't live too far from the canal and I have a fishing rod and a bicycle. So on quiet days, when I want to remove myself from the glare of life under the public spotlight, I dig up a handful of worms, pop on my cycle clips, or two generously proportioned rubber bands will do if you can't find your clips. If you can't find rubber bands, you can use string and if you can't find any string, you can push off and bother someone else, and off I go.

Incidentally a good way of finding worms is to dig for them in your garden. If you don't have a garden, ask a neighbour if you can dig for worms in their garden. Any reasonable neighbour should accede to your request. If they don't you can tell them to sod off from me.

Other famous celebrity fishermen are Hugo Furny-Whistable, the squirrel eater and Roger Daventry from the top pop group 'The Who'. (And yes that really is their name, before you ask).

It's funny you should mention Hugo-Furly-Whistable, because a few years ago he contacted me and asked if I'd be a part, a small part of his campaign for a chicken sanctuary, which I was highly delighted so to do.

Now I have to say until Hugo got in touch with me, I just used to buy chickens at the supermarket that were on offer. Like 'Six Chickens for a Pound!' etc. I never used to give any thought to their welfare and I, like Henry the Eighth before me, would wolf them down, hungrily, without a care in the world. Throwing the bones over my shoulder, where a Lady in waiting would be waiting to clear them up.

What Hugo told me about chickens froze me to

my marrowfat. He told me that apparently some people, and I can't name any names, because I don't know any of them, some people, put batteries in chickens. As I said to him, "That is scandalous!" I said. I said, "We all like to eat happy chickens for our dinner don't we? But that really has broke the camel for me, that has. And I don't say that easily."

And from that day forth I vowed not to eat any meat that doesn't have a smile on it's face. I know that doesn't sound much, but sometimes I'm in the supermarket for a couple of hours, going through the meat. Looking for anything that even half looks like half a half smile. Some vein of fat shaped like an upturned mouth, anything. Very often I have to have a tin of corned beef when I can't find anything, because corned beef isn't proper meat, so that doesn't count. It's like you can't sell ivory after thats newer than 1940 something. Which I also agree with. I'm a little bit of a pioneer when you think about it. Anyway it must cost a fortune putting batteries in them? Because you can't half get a lot of chickens in a hut. Unless they're rechargeable?

And that's what I do to relax. Fishing.

'CALLING INSPECTOR MAYNARD'

A NOVEL BY
COUNT ARTHUR STRONG

Maynard was looking out of the window, deep in
thought. It was a crystal clear winters morning
in December 1960 something. Ahead of him he
could see the steeples of Oxford and Cambridge.
He could never stop himself marvelling at
the wonderfulness of these hallowed halls of
learning.

At first he didn't hear the telephone ringing,
so deep in thought was he. And then he did.
He crossed the mahogany panelled interior of
his office, his shoes squeaking slightly on the
polished pitch pine floor, and arrived at his ash
desk. The desk was made out of 'ash'. Ash wood.
Not ash from a cigarette or a fire. I don't think
they can do that.

"Hello", he said into the mouthpiece, in an
educated voice. After he'd picked up the
telephone. Obviously.

"Maynard here"

For some moments he listened intently to whatever, whoever was talking to him said. Finally, when they'd stopped he spoke again.

"Thank you. That's very interesting. Be assured that if I ever want my windows doing, your company shall be my first port of call. Good day to you".

With that, he deftly hung up the telephone properly and returned to his vantage point at the window.

Suddenly there was a knock on the teak, four panelled Georgian door.

"Come, come", Maynard was heard to say.

The door opened and in walked Detective Sergeant Branchcombe, wearing ordinary clothes.

"What is it Branchcoombe?"

"Sorry to disturb you sir." He said in his thick West Country burr, "There's someone as want's to see you at the desk. I said you were not to be disturbed but they wouldn't take no for an answer, moi lover."

[308]

Maynard clicked his tongue, irritably.

"Did they give no indication of what it was about?"

"Theym zed summurt about they's from French Interpol" said Branchcoombe, shooting Maynard a look, laced with meaning.

Maynard wasn't having any of that and he shot Branchcoombe a better look back at himself. Branchcoome, looked away knowing he'd been bettered.

"Very well show whoever it is in."

"Proper job" said Branchcoombe, and was gone.

Maynard sighed, sometimes being the cleverest police detective in Oxford and Cambridge weighed heavily on his broad soldiers of his. He turned off the classical music he was listening to, I forgot to tell you about, probably 'The planet Suite', by Brahms or Beethoven, and sat down in his antique 'Captains' chair, made from the wood of an elm tree. It was the only chair he could sit on comfortably, since he got badly shot by a bullet hitting him. He shivered, involuntarily, as the memory of that night came back to him.

[309]

He had beeen having a large brandy in his
conservatory, when a sniper hidden in the woods,
which bordered his turn of the century Georgian
farmhouse, which had been in the family for
generations of years, shot him in the shoulder.
Smashing a pane of hand blown Georgian glass to
smithereens, which you can't get any more, and
knocking him clean off his feet.

The surgeon later told him that if it'd been
a millimetre in either direction, he wouldn't
have been telling him this. Because he would
be dead. Shot through the heart by person or
persons unknown. However, the bullet passed
clean through the soft tissue of his scapula. He
absentmindedly massaged his shoulder, because
that's where a scapula is.

His reverie was interrupted by a knock on
another door

His reverie was interrupted by another knock on
the door. The door opened and in came Sergeant
Branchcoombe again. Behind him followed a
French looking woman. She was tall, slim, with
mischievous eyes that Maynard found hard to
read. A bit like 'The Old Curiosity Shop'.

"Mamaselle Dupont from Interpol, my lover",
Branchcoombe utttered.

"Very pleased to meet you, coffee?

"Zat wurd be acceptable. Sank you"

"Get us two coffee's Branchcoombe wurd you"
Maynard ejaculated.

"Proper job", replied Branchcoombe and left the
room.

"Please sit down Mamselle Dupont".

"Sank you. Please call me Bernice"

"What a beautiful name," uttered Maynard,
urbanely.

"Sink you".

"Would you be appier if we conducted zis
converstation in your own tongue", Maynard
said, in word perfect French. He had mastered
in French at Oxford and Cambridge and had a first
degree in it.

"You spik very gut French, but it not necessary
sank you", Bernice said coquettishly?

There was a knock and the door opened for one
final last time in this chapter because it's
getting on my nerves. Branchcoombe came in
carefully carrying a tray which had coffee
things on it for two. He set the coffee making
implementalia down on Maynard's hogmanay desk
and withdrew. From the room, silently, not
saying anything this time.

Maynard deftly poured two cups of coffee each
out. He then waited until Bernard picked up a
cup, had a sip and put it down again before he
spoke.

"So, what can I do for Interpol", he said.

Without speaking, Bernard, Bernice tossed a file
across the table at him, which she had in her
bag. She had a bag with her.

Maynard raised an eyebrow and looked at her. She
met his gaze and looked back at him. There was
fire in those eyes he remembered thinking. He
held her gaze for a moment or two. Eventually he
nodded, I'm not sure why, and looked down at the
file. Taking his time he opened it. He read it.
When he finished, he sat back and let out a low
even whistle.

"I presume your intelligence is sound?"

"Yezz", she replied. Her eyes never once leaving his face.

Maynard put both his elbows on his wooden desk and then put his finger tips together. He sucked his cheeks in, the ones in his head, deep in thought while he processed what he'd just read. Eventually he spoke, and when he did this time his voice had taken on a new edge. "So let's get this straight Bernard, what Interflora is saying is that the Mafia will attempt to assassinate the Prime Minister of England at the G8 summit, at six o'clock tonight. Correct?"

"Yes", she responded to his question. "Zat is correct".

I'm not going to do any more of this at the moment because it's getting on my nerves how she talks, and I might make her not come from France, and I don't want to give the story away. Because I don't want someone seeing it lying on a desk at Faber and Faber and Faber and copying it and then cracking on they made it up. T S Elliot or someone. But you get the gist of how

[313]

good the book will be? I mean there could be
car chases and poisonings, and a fight in a cable
car. I've got enough ideas for dozens of these
books. And then there's the television side of
it all. Now Morse is dead ITV'll be on the look
out for another one. As far as I know there's
never been an Inspector Maynard before, so tell
them they need to get in quick, before someone
else comes up with it. That's the name of the
game in this business, 'The next big thing'.
His first name's Enterprise. Tell them that.
Enterprise Maynard. Never mind 'Endeavour',
which is a ridiculous name for a person called
it.

THE END

Chapter 41

MOBY DICK

After the bleak years of the second world war,
which I outlined thoroughly in an earlier
chapter, (It was the war that Hitler did, if you've
forgotten?), we all desperately needed cheering
up a bit. A young entrepreneur called Billy
Butlin had an idea. His idea was to transform
the notion of the family holiday by building
holiday camps like they had in 'Hi-de-hi'. Thus
was laid the foundation stone of what we
affectionately know today as 'Butlins'.

Now over the years Butlin has been a home to
many top stars, including my good myself. And a
lot of todays celebrities got their starts there.
Stars such as Des O'Connor, Orville, Mike and
Bernie Winters, Joan Littlewood, Arthur Mullard,
Lawrence Olivier and Spencer Tracy are just
some of the celebrities I can remember. To be
honest I don't think they all went to Butlin.
But it doesn't really matter anyway, if they did
or not, because I'm using them illustratively.

John Geilgud and Ralph Richardson are another
two I've just remembered. And John Nettles off
Bergerac. It's amazing if you put your mind to
it, just how many you can remember. Why don't you
try remembering celebrities at home? See how
many you can come up with? You could call it 'The
Count Arthur Strong Celebrity Challenge'.

But you can't use the ones I've just mentioned.
That would be cheating. And cheats never beat!
I was playing Monopoly once with someone who
will have to remain nameless who cheated. You
wouldn't believe who it was if I told you. He
looked a lot like Christopher Timothy, if that's
not too much of a clue. It was his turn and he
moved the hat on to 'Go'.

I said,"What are you playing at?".

He said, "What?"

I said, "You're on Mayfair. Not Go. That's Mayfair
with one hotel on. Two thousand pounds please".

He said, "I'm not on Mayfair".

I said, "You are".

He said, "I'm not!"

I said, "Look, what did you throw?"

He said, "Ten"

I said "You didn't".

He said, "I did. A four and a six. Four and six is ten".

I said, "I know what a four and six is, thank you". I said, "Listen, if you threw ten, that would mean you were on 'Go To Jail' to end up on 'Go'. So I've caught you out there haven't I?"

He said, "Oh I'll take my go again then because of all this confusion".

I said, "You will not take your bloody go again! You should be in jail. Not roaming the streets free.

He said, "Oh shut up!"

I said, "Don't you tell me to shut up".

He said, "Well don't tell me to shut up".

I said, "I don't think I did".

He said, "Well you did".

I said, "Alright, I'll tell you what, clever Dick, I'm going to read this back, and if I didn't tell you to shut up in it then I want a full apology.

And I've just read it back and nowhere in this chapter did I tell you to shut up. So come on then, apologise. Wherever you are.

CHAPTER

TWELVE GOOD MEN (AND WOMEN) AND TRUE

On Saturday the something, of, I think it might
have been January 1990 something, I stood up
in my hall after having bended down to pick
up that mornings post. Amongst the usual raft
of fan letters was secreted one brown manilla
envelope. Intrigued I stuck my finger in it's flap
and tore it open. I pulled out the piece of paper
from within, and proceeded to read what I'm about
to write.

It said. 'This letter is to confirm that you are
required to attend the Law Courts of the Old
Bailey this day of our Lord 1990 something. If
you for any reason consider yourself illegible
would you please contact the clerk of the court
forthwith'.

Unfortunately I was illegible for jury duty
owing to something I can't go into, which was
more of a misunderstanding than anything.
Which was a shame because I'd have liked to have

written something about here. It would have been the perfect place for it wouldn't it?

I wonder what the case was they wanted me to preside over? Lord Lucan possibly? Or 10 Rillington Place? When Richard Attenborough murdered all those women. I don't think they ever got him for that, Richard Attenborough, did they? They hung John Hurt for it. Which when you think about it, it didn't do his career any harm did, being hung? He went on from strength to strength.

They obviously wouldn't have asked someone like me to do parking fines. It would have been a waste of who I am. They'd probably get some minor celebrity to do motor related offences. Maybe someone like Mike Brewer and Ed China off 'Wheeler Dealers'. Because that's their thing motoring isn't it. That would make sense. That's what they should do. Get all the experts off the telly. If it's a property issue get Phil and Kirsty off, 'Location, Location, Location. Or him off 'Grand Designs', that's always chopping herbs up in people's kitchens. I'll speak to someone about that. *who?*

I'll tell you something I've noticed though, how
many times do you hear, when there's a trial
on, that the jury has retired? It happens all
the time. Why for goodness sake don't they just
get younger people. It's not 'rocket salad is
it'? The money they must waste. And now I heard
on the radio, yesterday I think it was, that
Eddie Stobart's lorry drivers are going to be
solicitors as well. How's that going to work. What
if they've got a case on in Liverpool say, and
he's stuck in Newcastle, with a full load because
his tachometer says he's got to have a two hour
break? Honestly that will just make a mockery
of the legal system if you ask me. We'll be the
laughing stock of the rest of the world.

They say our legal system is admired the world
over don't they and then in the next breath
they're making a nonsense of everything we hold
dear to ourselves. You couldn't make it up could
you?

CHAPTER

THE FINAL CURTAIN

Handwritten margin notes:
Soap
Stamps
Liver
Onion
Barely wate
Plasters
Unexplai

It was 1990 something or 1960 something,
it depends which way up you do the six,
approximately 5.17am in the morning. I woke
suddenly from a deep sleep. As my both eyes
accustomed themselves to the light, or dark
really, if I'm being accurate, I could make out
the familiar images of my roomful of possessions,
accrued over the years. Possessions that had
come to mean so very much to me. Like a chair or
a sideboard or a cuckoo clock, possibly, and I
though to myself, 'If I . . .

Suddenly this sentence was interrupted by a
noise coming from downstairs. I quickly realised
that my house was being broken into by anywhere
between four and twelve people. Probably armed.

I silently applied my dressing gown to myself,
walked to the door and listened. Yes! There was
definitely a number of people involved in the
felony taking place in my downstairs. What to do?

[322]

I thought for a bit longer then I made up my mind. With the famous Count Arthur steely resolve, I decided that . . .

If you want to find out what Count Arthur Strong did next, then could I suggest that you buy volume number two of his wonderful memoirs of his, when it comes out, 'Through It All I Always Laughed Again', and it will all be in there up to date. Or I might not do it completely up to date because I want to get at least another volume or two out of this, after that one.

And further more, can I just say that it really is terrific value for money, my life. I don't know how much they're charging for these books but they could double the price and it would still be sound economics to get it. It really is a very astute investment all round, books of mine. The Institute of Fiscal Studies would probably be right behind that assertion. In fact I might phone them up this afternoon and get a quote from them to put in here. If they're on the phone. And another plus is, my memoirs would be equally as impressive, displayed as a conversation piece on your shelving units or on a glass topped coffee table. If you've got one of those? I have no way of knowing that. So you see, you don't even have to read my book to impress people. Although my suggestion would be that you do read it because you'll be missing out on all my wonderful memories. Or at least read this bit. But as long as you buy it that's the important thing. I'm not one of these authors that likes to tell you what to do when you buy a book. I believe in freedom of expression. And that's what you get with 'Through It All I've Always Laughed'.

'THROUGH IT ALL I'VE ALWAYS LAUGHED'

AKNOWLEDGEMENT'S

I have so many people to thank for making this
memoir of mine possible. After me obviously,
because I did all the donkey work on it. And
I do hope I don't offend donkeys or anyone by
leaving them out because of space constraints.
As I stated at the beginning without my mother
and father having physical relations with each
other I wouldn't be here, so I'd like to thank them
for that first and foremost, wherever they went,
for not taking precautions,.

Next I'd like to thank my publishers, Faber and
Faber and Faber, who's unwavering support and
encouragement I'm expecting any day now.

Next in line, step forward   my editor,
who's marvellous editing really was something
else. We really did develop a wonderful rapport
between us. And I have to say in working with
him, or her, or them, it really came home to me
just how inportant it is to have a good one of
those, to do whatever their job is for you. It is

[325]

a bit shrouded in mystery is editing. All very
'cloak and dagger' and I'm assured he/her/they,
did a thoroughly alright job. Although I'm not
reading the book back to find out. It was bad
enough writing it in the first place. Only joking.
It was a daily joy. (I would just say, if you don't
enjoy the book, that it was marvellous before
I handed it on to whoever edited it. So they've
probably spoilt it and I'm furious with them
about that. And on your behalf I will speak to
them and tell them not to do that again. Unless
you've got it out of the library? In which case
you're on your own, because you've not paid for
it have you? Sponging of us authors! So if you
didn't enjoy it, you can go and whistle!).

Next, I want to thank the marvellous people I've
met throughout my life that all played a part
in my literary opus. Don't worry I'm not going
to name them all because again, that would take
ages and I'd have to read the book back to make
a list up. And as I've already stated it's not fair
to ask me to do that. I wish people would stop
that. I'm quite keen to finish doing this book
asap. I'm a writer. There's nothing in my contract
about reading anything I've written back. I was

most particular about that. However if one of you wanted to take that task upon yourself, for no renumeration, that would be alright. I know there are peculiar people around that do that sort of thing when they read books. Anyway I'm not really bothered whether you do or not. I'm not doing it. I've put my shift in on this. So it's just a collective thank you to the lot of them, in one lump as it were. And as I say, no offence intended to, Barry Cryer, for instance, for not mentioning him or people like him here. The use of the name Barry Cryer in this passage was for illustrative purposes only.

And finally, and I am genuinely choked up as I write this, I want to thank you, the general pubic for buying this book. Whether you bought it to read, or just to display, to impress friends and family, the fact that you did one of those, means so very much to me and I honestly can't wait until you buy the next one, when I've written it.

So ladies and gentlemen it's time for me to bid you farewell, and can I leave you with this thought, that no matter what, no matter who, no matter why, 'Through It All I've Always Laughed'.

[327]

Stamps.!!!

First published in Great Britain in 2013
by Faber and Faber Limited
Bloomsbury House
74–77 Great Russell Street
London WC1B 3DA

Typeset by Faber and Faber Ltd
Printed in England by CPI Group (UK) Ltd, Croydon, CR0 4YY

A CIP record for this book
is available from the British Library

ISBN 978–0–571–30338–0

2 4 6 8 9 7 5 3 1